BUSINESS-BUILDING REFERRALS

Play Your A-Game and Become
a Networking Super Star

BUSINESS-BUILDING REFERRALS

Play Your A-Game and Become a Networking Super Star

LORRAINE LANE

Lorraine Lane
Lane Business Consulting
17953 Hunting Bow Circle, Suite 102
Lutz, FL 33558

www.BusinessBuildingReferrals.com

ISBN: 978-1482334623

Printed in the United States of America

First Printing 2013

Cover and interior design by TotenCreative
Author photograph by Ragan Jenkins

PRAISE FOR *BUSINESS-BUILDING REFERRALS*

"Everyone wants a referral-based business because we all know that the best prospects come from referrals. They are less skeptical, cost less and are more comfortable to acquire. But mastering the art of having a steady stream of referrals is something else indeed. Lorraine Lane knows. She's studied it, tested what works—and what doesn't. She's taught it and refined it into a science. And she's sharing it with you now in this book. If you want to learn something well, find a master and listen and practice carefully. Lorraine is that master. And this book will put you on the path to mastering business-building referrals. I highly recommend it."

—Michael Angier
Founder and president, SuccessNet.org
Author of several books on the Science of Successful Thinking

"This book is an easy read, while being substantial and 'meaty' at the same time. Ms. Lane is direct and insistent in the direction she gives, but never overbearing. I found her exercises to be excellent, producing powerful learning. Chapter Ten presents a straightforward and especially powerful concept—one that was new to me, and that I have already begun to implement. It will produce fine results for readers of *Business-Building Referrals*."

—Jay Michlin
Retired Technology Executive

"I love this book! I'm a past participant in Lorraine's *A-Game Program*: the tactics she teaches have helped me to be intentional both about *giving* and *getting* referrals. I'm proud to say that most of my business comes from referrals. This book is a study guide to help you grow your business. Actively play your 'business game' the A-Game way—and you will win all the way to the bank."

—Laura Woodard, President
GrassRoots Marketing Group, Inc.
Sales and Marketing Consultants
Tampa, FL

"*Business-Building Referrals* provides the foundation to maximize networking activities and enhance the steps to reach potential clients. Lorraine demonstrates the experience in building successful networks from the ground up and her A-Game method provides the basic tenets to successful revenue growth. Lorraine's direct consultation has provided a great impact on our organization."

—Richard Semancik, COO
Paxen Learning Corporation
Melbourne, FL

"In *Business-Building Referrals*, Lorraine Lane describes the practical details of positioning oneself with the right trajectory to create a thriving business. Working in small metro area markets, where most people live and work, making connections is imperative. Building on her own struggles and experience, Lorraine lays out an honest and straight-forward program for conquering internal and external barriers to success. She weaves the practical realities of being your own sales person and business developer with concrete actions that can take the reader from bewildered to benefiting in business."

—Charles Armiger, VP Program Development
SpeedInfo
San Jose, CA

"I really enjoyed *Business-Building Referrals.* I didn't expect it to be so engaging, as the topic didn't seem to apply to me. However, it totally held my interest and I kept finding myself saying, 'yeah, that's great advice for these other situations, too.' Lorraine's writing style is friendly and down to earth, very easy to understand, yet professional. This book will be a gem for anyone serious about growing their business. There's no doubt a lot of work to be done, but Lorraine has broken it down into manageable pieces that will give confidence to even the faintest of hearts."

—Carolyn Joslin PHR
Southwest Florida Water Management District

KUDOS FOR LORRAINE AND HER A-GAME PROGRAM

"Lorraine's *A-Game Program* had a major impact on my business practices, marketing attitude and—most importantly—on the results to my bottom line. The A-Game Program of Business-Building Referrals is about so much more than referrals: it encompasses how you *think* about referrals, the *actions* you take to build business relationships, and the *creation* of an environment that is beneficial to both you and your referral partners. I love this program and recommend it to everyone I know who has clients or customers, and anyone who wants to develop a bigger community based on mutual interests."

—Pegotty Cooper, FASAE, IOM
Leadership and Career Coach
Tampa, FL

"The *A-Game Program* is a 'must do' for every small business owner. In fact, the program was so valuable to me that I participated a second time. I now have a solid base of referral partners and a steady stream of clients. I've become much better at networking as a result of the A-Game Program: I ask questions and I listen…instead of launching into a commentary about my business and myself. I've learned to be present with my clients and listen to their needs and desires. Several clients have told me how much they appreciate the fact that I listen to them. The A-Game of Business-Building Referrals is a proven strategy and my participation in it has made my business both more enjoyable and more profitable."

— Dennis Esber
Master Printer
Point To Point Printing, Inc.
Lutz, FL

"The four As of the *A-Game of Business-Building Referrals* caused a big turnaround in my thinking. I learned that building a referral business is not just about networking. It's about making connections when you network, and then building relationships with those whose businesses I can help, and who can help me."

—Cheryl Herman
Land O' Lakes, FL
LifeVantage

"Working with Lorraine Lane in her capacity as a coach has been a transformative experience. We met my initial goals of vastly improved communication with colleagues in a high-stress environment and more effective collaborative skills, in my work as an administrator and as a teacher. Now she is helping to catapult me in the direction of my dreams! I recommend Lorraine Lane to people who want to raise the bar of their performance in the workplace and enhance effectiveness in all aspects of their lives."

—Susan Taylor-Lennon
Chair, Arts and Theatre
University of Tampa

"My participation in the *A-Game of Business-Building Referrals* resulted in a mind shift. I used to attend networking events and think to myself, *how can my business benefit from this event today?* Now when I attend events, I ask myself, *how can my business be of benefit to attendees at this event today?* This simple shift allowed me to relax at these events and enjoy networking: getting to know people, asking questions, and then listening. When I enjoy something, I want to do it more often, so now I seek out more networking opportunities, which ultimately increases my business opportunities."

—Fran Powers
Founder, Powerstories Theatre
"Staging true stories to open minds and hearts"

"Last year I had the pleasure of participating in a ten-week program that focused on your referral A-Game, facilitated by Lorraine Lane. As a very busy financial advisor, I am always leery about committing my time to anything but my practice. As it turned out, Lorraine's program was a surprising game-changer for me. Over the course of the class, Lorraine really taught me to be much more aware of my surroundings, my clients' goals, and most importantly, how I was interacting with others. The ultimate benefit I received is the ability to truly listen. My listening skills have been refined and as a result, I've enjoyed increased client acquisition, and have been able to uncover more opportunities in my practice. The enhancement of my listening skills has been a gift. I recommend Lorraine and her A-Game Program to anyone who is looking for a game changer in their career or business."

—*Eliot Dylan Marr*
CEO, Marr Financial Group

"My wife met Lorraine Lane at a networking event we were attending, and immediately sought me out in the crowd to introduce me. With the down-turn in the economy, my law practice was suffering, as was just about every other business we knew. Lorraine introduced herself as someone who helped businesses like mine to grow. This was something my firm definitely needed. Lawyer advertising has become big business, but our law firm is small and focuses on personal referrals as its main source of clientele. I hired Lorraine shortly after our meeting to help 're-grow' our business. Lorraine incorporated her 'four As' and helped motivate my partners, my staff, and me to become more aware and attentive to the business. It wasn't long before we began to redevelop referral partners, increase referral sources, and generally enjoy a revitalization of our practice. I know first-hand that the *A-Game* is a winning formula to improve business, increase revenues, and more importantly generate a long-term referral base. I thank my wife Andrea for making this valuable introduction and Lorraine for helping take my business to the next level."

—Craig A. Laporte, Esquire
Proly, Laporte & Mulligan, P.A.
Port Richey, FL

To all the players of the A-Game.

Please be sure to visit
www.BusinessBuildingReferrals.com/readers-only
and register to receive Lorraine's newsletter
and be notified about offers
exclusively for Lorraine's readers.

CONTENTS

FOREWORD

Hello Dear Reader,

Will you play big? Or will you play safe? *That* is the question.

Coach Dave Buck here. I'm excited that you're reading this great book by my longtime friend and colleague, Coach Lorraine Lane. Building a solid, referral-based business—and becoming a networking super star—is one of the most challenging and important games you'll ever learn to play. This book will teach you how to do just that. It's worthy of your time and effort to work on your A-Game because the potential rewards are massive.

Why do I say this? Here's a BIG truth: The fundamental purpose of the game of life is to contribute to the lives of others. Nearly every opportunity you have to contribute will come from your network. This includes your business, career, community and even love and romance. Your network is your connection to the greater community and this is where everything happens.

Here's a great example from my life: In my thirties I was enjoying a successful career as a computer systems analyst, but I was yearning to do something bigger with one of my lifelong passions, soccer. At the time I was also a Yoga teacher. Once a month we had an informal networking dinner for all the Yoga teachers in the area. At one such meeting I was speaking with a woman and sharing a powerful story about my desire do something with my passion for soccer. It turns out that she was on the athletic staff at Seton Hall University and she knew that the men's soccer team was looking for two assistant coaches. WOW. The Head Coach at Seton Hall was Manny Schellscheidt, a Hall of Fame player, coach and soccer legend! This was an opportunity I never would have dared to even dream about. The next thing I knew, I was sitting in Coach Manny's office being interviewed for the job, and eventually I was hired. I held that position for 15 years and it's one of the highlights of my life. I am so grateful for my network.

Another amazing networking success story from my life includes Coach Lorraine. She was a student in our Coach Training program at CoachVille, and when we decided to put together a team of coaching leaders from various major cities, Coach Lorraine stepped up and took control in Tampa, Florida. Lorraine came to the networking retreat we hosted and played big by sharing and teaching others how to become leaders in their communities through networking. I was amazed by her generosity.

A few months later, through her Chamber of Commerce connections, Lorraine was referred to a company in need of customer service training. As professional coaches, Lorraine and I are focused on helping individuals and organizations who have the desire to step up their business game. (It's no secret that a professional coach helps you play a better game.) Lorraine knew she could help this company, but not in the way they thought. When she met with the representatives of the company, Lorraine boldly suggested to the management team that they needed coaching leadership training. The company leaders were intrigued by her idea: Lorraine made a proposal, and it was accepted. She brought me in as a collaborator and together we conducted a one-year coach training program that transformed the business from a struggling company to a "Coach Approach" organization worth millions of dollars. It's one of the most successful ventures either of us has ever accomplished in terms of both long-term financial results and personal fulfillment.

Think of all the networking that enabled Coach Lorraine to pull that venture together: She networked her way to a position of visibility in both her local business community and the coach training community, and pulled those networks together to create a winning team.

With such great rewards as the prize for winning the networking and referral game, it's only natural that the challenges are also great. This is where this book comes into play: To win at this game, you must possess skills and a game plan. But the most important tool you need is awareness of your own inner doubts and fears–your inner game–because that will be the biggest challenge you'll have to overcome as you build your network.

Like many others, you probably have a strong desire to play big, go out in the world, make a contribution and build a business. That's why you're reading this book. What you may not be aware of is that you have an equally strong human imperative to hide and play safe. This "survival instinct" part of our human nature is what makes life so interesting. If it were easy to just go out in the world and make your mark, it would not be a game worth playing.

It's a BIG challenge and in the face of a BIG challenge, you need a great coach.

You know how some people seem to be just "natural" at doing something while others really have to put in concentrated effort to get results? Most of the time, it's the folks who really had to put in the effort who become the best coaches. This describes Coach Lorraine perfectly: I know from personal experience that she is *not* a natural networker. At our networking retreat, Coach Lorraine revealed that earlier in her life, she was a nun who lived in a Cloistered Monastery. WHAT?? Talk about playing it safe by hiding out! You can't get any more hidden than living in a monastery.

When Coach Lorraine made up her mind to leave the monastery, she set herself on a path to make her mark in the world. She faced a lot of inner doubt and fear along the way, but she did it. Her journey from total silence to president of her Chamber of Commerce was long and challenging, and qualifies Lorraine to guide you on *your* journey to playing your A-Game and becoming a networking super star.

If you're reading this book, then you probably have a desire to be considered a person of influence in the communities in which you interact, and to make a difference in the world. This book will give you some great tools and action plans. Then you have to get out there and play the game. *Your A-Game.* When you run into challenges "on the field"—which you will—make sure you have a great Coach like Lorraine on your side.

Coach Dave Buck, Master Certified Coach, MBA
CEO, CoachVille.com
"We Teach the World to Coach! All in Service
of Humanity Flourishing"

MY STORY

I'm an ex-corporate-employee-turned-small-business-owner, (X-CORP for short). All of us who are corporate drop-outs—for whatever reason—have our stories to tell. I want to tell you mine because it's the foundation on which I built my business, and on which I wrote this book. Some of it may even sound familiar to you.

After fifteen (mostly happy) years in the high-tech industry, I was shocked when I was given the dreaded pink slip. It was 1995. For the first time in my professional life, I was jobless. *How could this happen? How DID this happen?* I worked for a well-known high-tech company. I had totally devoted myself to this organization for fifteen years. And now this. Two weeks earlier, I had received a two- level promotion with stock options. Then corporate headquarters lowered the boom. Thanks to budget cuts, our entire department was laid off. Overnight. I had thought—as I'm sure many corporate ladder-climbers do—that I would work for many years, build upon my successes and eventually receive a coveted gold watch at my retirement dinner. I spent nine of my fifteen years in Human Resources and the last six years working on a project for the vice president of Customer Service. (At the request of the vice president, I spearheaded an initiative to develop competency models and training for managers across the United States.) My group and I accomplished great things, and I know we added to the company's bottom line.

Not too long after being laid off, I received a phone call asking if I was free to do some training for CCL, the *Center for Creative Leadership*. While at my high-tech company, I'd been certified to facilitate SYMLOG, a team-building program, and CCL needed someone with that certification. I must admit luck was on my side. I breathed a sigh of relief agreed to do the project on a freelance basis. During the course of the program, I was asked by a couple of the participants (who themselves were corporate managers) if I was available to facilitate this same program for their organizations. Fortunately, I'd thought ahead and had had some business cards printed up, so I handed each of these managers a card and invited them to give me a call.

Meanwhile, I diligently continued to look for a job. Those corporate managers did call me, and I happily went off to facilitate programs for them. And so it went: While I continued to pour my heart and soul into looking for a job, I accepted freelance facilitation gigs. One evening, about six months into my freelancing and job hunting routine, my husband and I were in the kitchen and I was combing through employment ads in the paper. My husband was figuring something out on a calculator. He looked up from what he was doing and said, "You have your own business. You've replaced your corporate income!" I was flabbergasted. I didn't believe it. I didn't want to believe it. I wanted to be in the corporate world forever, just like I'd planned. I didn't believe the workshop facilitation I was doing constituted a real *business*. It was a *side job*. I pooh-poohed my husband's suggestion that I had a business, put my head down, and worked even harder at finding a new job…all the while taking those "side jobs."

Finally, eighteen months after being let go from the high-tech company, I interviewed for, and was offered, a new position. I jumped at it, but my excitement was short-lived. The job—and my manager—were both nightmares. I quit after two months.

Back at home once again, I shifted my mindset: I still wasn't willing to admit I was "in business" for myself, but I did comfort myself with the knowledge that at least I could add to the household income by doing the training sessions. I began to wonder how I could get more of this kind of work, and so I became a student. I read everything I could get my hands on about how to acquire more business. I didn't have a business plan (because after all, I wasn't in business!) and I didn't have a marketing plan, but everything I read told me that the way to get business is to network. So I tried. I decided I would become a networking super star.

I'd read about a local women's networking group and decided it would be a great place to start. On the given Wednesday morning, I suited up, resolutely piled into my car, and backed out of the driveway. Then I put my car in "drive," pulled forward, and went right back into my garage. I was terrified. I couldn't do it! Ask me to teach a workshop for 100 people . . . no problem. But don't ask me to introduce myself to a group of women I've never seen before in my entire life and tell them what I do. That evening at the dinner table, my husband and daughter asked how the networking meeting went. All I could say was, "Don't ask." I knew that attending these meetings was *the way* for me to find work, so I was determined to go to the next one, no matter what it took. So, the next Wednesday, I made it all the way to the parking lot of the building where the meeting was being held . . . and then I turned around and drove home. "Come on, Lorraine!" I chided myself. What was wrong with me? I swore to myself that I would go to that meeting the following week, no matter what.

The day of the next meeting I got off to a good start. I drove to the meeting location and parked my car in the lot. I was sitting in my car, my heart beating rapidly out of sheer terror, when a knock on my window scared me half to death. I looked up to see a woman (all suited up just like me) who asked, "Are you here for the networking meeting?" When I responded yes, she suggested we go in together and said she'd introduce me. I was trapped. I had to do it this time. When everyone in the room took turns introducing themselves, I wanted to crawl under the table. I didn't know how to introduce myself because I wasn't *in business* like all these other women. By the time I left the meeting, my suit was soaking wet. I went home, put the suit in the pile for the dry cleaner, and cried all morning.

The next morning, I got up, gathered all the books I'd been reading about networking, and piled them all around me. I knew I needed a "thirty-second commercial," so I worked on it for an entire day. I went to the meeting the following week with my thirty-second commercial on a 3"x5" card. I was still shaking when I introduced myself, but it was easier with my little card in hand. I vowed to keep going to those networking meetings, and I did. Meanwhile, I read everything I could get my hands on about building a business. Gradually, I started conducting classes for the group based on everything I was reading. I helped a lot of the members get their businesses moving by teaching them how to market themselves and how to sell. I didn't realize it at the time, but I was essentially coaching these women for free. Not only was I was very good at it, but it was easy for me: helping and teaching these women was a way to combine my passion for imparting knowledge with my corporate experience as a trainer.

My "business" was really getting off the ground when my husband was recruited for a great position in California. It just so happened I was freelancing with a company that had a California location, so I spoke to company representatives about doing work for them on the west coast. They were thrilled. My husband and I packed our bags. In spite of having that freelance work in California, I decided to look for a job there as well, because I knew no one and had no network in California. I found a great position that lasted for two years. Soon after, a colleague approached me to partner with him in a new business venture, working with a major financial institution. Once again, I jumped at the chance. I poured my heart and soul—and some of my money—into this venture. One day, I went to work and found the doors bolted shut– and my "partner" nowhere to be found. To this day, I haven't heard from him, and I lost quite a bit of my own money in his company. Big lessons learned!

This was not the best of times for my family: My husband had been laid off, I had no more work, I'd lost a lot of money, and I hadn't seen my daughter in a year., So we decided to move back home to Florida. It had been eight years since I'd gotten that first pink slip, and at this point in my life, I knew I was finished with trying to find another job. Back in Florida, I decided to build my business again. I knew exactly how to do it: I had read all the right books and was ready to jump in with both feet.

INTRODUCTION

Fifteen years have passed since the day I made the monumental decision to drive a stake in the ground and move ahead with building my own business. Today, I help X-CORPs and other small business owners who want to build businesses of their own: I do this by working with business owners and coaching them one-on-one. I also facilitate a ten-week program, the A-Game of Business-Building Referrals. That's what this book is all about: *building a business . . . your business.* The A-Game is a business-building strategy that involves growing your business based on true, relationship-based referrals.

As a small business owner myself, I've been where you are. If you're an X-CORP, know that I've experienced both the pain and the pleasure of the corporate world, just like you. And, I've experienced the ups and downs of building a small business. This book is for every small business owner, whether or not you're an X-CORP.

Because I've had a successful career in the corporate world, I know how to do what I'm told. So that's what I did when I started my business. There's a plethora of books, classes, and people, all claiming to guide you to success in building your small business. I read those books, attended the classes and consulted with experts on how to get clients. It quickly became apparent to me that I had to become a networking super star: all I had to do was attend lots of networking meetings, and other business owners would refer new business to me. Compared to my work in the corporate world, this was going to be a walk in the par—or so I thought. I jumped in and did what all the books, classes and experts told me to do: I networked. There were days when I went to networking functions for breakfast, lunch and dinner. I even joined one of those closed networking groups in which referrals are mandatory.

But it didn't work. After four years of membership in the same networking group and dutifully participating in the weekly meetings, I realized something HUGE was missing: My ROI (Return on Investment). Remember, I'd come up the ranks in corporate America. I know that if you cannot show an ROI, a project isn't worth undertaking. I quickly put pen to paper and figured out the return on the investment of time and money I'd put into this group for the past four years. Can you guess the outcome? *I wasn't even breaking even.* My net result was a giant goose egg. I quit the next day.

Today, I own a true referral-based business and, not to boast, but I consider myself to be a networking super star. That's not to say that I don't do any marketing. I have a business plan and a marketing plan, and I follow them, but most of my effort—when it comes to getting new clients—is in cultivating relationships with my referral partners. I can honestly say that 80 percent of my business comes directly from these relationships. Nine times out of ten, when one of my referral partners sends someone to me, it results in money in the bank. I now have the business I used to dream of.

How the A-Game Came Into Being

Those of you who read books written by business "gurus" know there's plenty of noise out there about networking and referrals. I, too, had read all of those books, yet I still struggled with networking. I started asking myself questions about networking: *What am I doing wrong? What am I aware of as I network? What am I overlooking?* I recorded all of my answers in a notebook.

Within a few months, I had several notebooks filled with my thoughts, answers to my questions, and observations about networking. I decided to use my findings as the foundation for a workshop I called "Business-Building Referrals," which is, not coincidentally, the title of this book. Participants of my early workshops made progress in their networking, and they kept asking for more. Over the course of a few years, my workshop evolved into what it is today: the ten-week A-Game program.

You might be wondering, *why the "A-Game?"* It came to me one day while reading the newspaper. I saw the words "A-Game" in an ad. I thought of the foundational principles of my workshop: **A**wareness and **A**ttention, **A**uthenticity, **A**ttraction and **A**ction. I know that in the world of sports, "to bring your A-Game" means athletes must play with their best attitudes and highest levels of skill. Whether it's playing soccer, baseball or some other sport, the coach tells his team to bring their A-Game, meaning if the players were given a grade for their performance in the game, they would receive an "A." That's exactly what you and I need to do in business: we need to be able to give ourselves an "A" for each and every performance.

If building a referral-based business and becoming a networking super star sounds like something you want to do, then I congratulate you for buying this book. More than a decade of experience—my own experience in building my business and the experience of my clients—has gone into the writing of this book. A word of caution: This is not a step-by-step, how-to book. This book will certainly reveal how to go about building a referral-based business, and I'll be giving you some steps for how do it. However, this book is more about the foundational principles and qualities that will bring you success as you network, nurture your referral partners and grow your business. I provide you with a discovery process that will work for you based on *who you are* and *what you're willing to do*.

We'll begin in Chapter One with the prerequisites—*my* prerequisites—for building a business. In Chapter Two, we'll talk all about referrals: exactly what they are, and why you should use them to build your business. Then we'll jump right into the A-Game—in Chapters Three through Six—the four principles that are the underpinning of business-building referrals. Next, in Chapter Seven, we'll talk about building your network. I think you're going to love Chapter Eight, where I reveal my number one strategy for building a referral-based business. In Chapter Nine, I'll share my perspective on traditional networking and becoming a networking super star.

One quick note: throughout this book, I use the term "clients." You might use the term "customers," or you may even have "patients." Feel free to substitute the term that is most natural and comfortable for you as you read.

What I want is for you to discover that certain special something that is unique to you, and whatever it is that brings out the A-Player in you. My challenge to you is to bring your A-Game to your business each and every day and to become a networking super star. Are you ready to get off the couch and get in the game? Well, then, turn the page, and let's go.

CHAPTER ONE

THE PREREQUISITES
Walk before you run

Before you take even the first step on your journey of business-building referrals, you must have your ducks in a row. All your ducks. I categorize these "ducks" into three groups:

1. Basics

2. Mindset

3. The Four **A**s

Since this book is all about referrals, I'm going to assume you've got the "basics" already covered for you and your business. The basics include (but are certainly not limited to) creating and developing a proven concept for a service or product to sell, a business plan, a business checking account, working capital, etc. There are hundreds upon hundreds of books written on the basics of starting a business, along with a wealth of information on the Internet. Be sure you have the basics under control.

In this chapter, I want to talk about your mindset. When I meet with a potential client, or when I begin a new ten-week program, there are four main areas I cover immediately:

1. How serious are you?

2. How busy are you?

3. How do you spend your time?

4. How willing are you to leave your comfort zone?

Let's take a look at each of these areas.

How Serious Are You?

One of the first questions I ask both my individual clients and my program participants is, "How Serious Are You?" On a scale of 1-10, with 10 being as serious as you possibly can be with a willingness to do whatever it takes, how serious are you about building a successful business? I'd like you to take a minute to answer this question for yourself right now. Be perfectly honest. Take your number and write it down in the margin of this book. I ask this question because I come in contact with so many small business owners who don't seem to be serious about their businesses. Building and sustaining a business is as serious and fun a game as you'll ever play. To win the game, you have to be a full-out player. You must practice every day. Are you in? All the way in? Half-way won't work. As an X-CORP, I know you're accustomed to working hard, but don't be fooled into thinking that owning a small business will be easier than being a corporate employee. In the corporate world, momentum happens automatically. You have direction from above (unless, of course, you're the CEO, but even then you report to a Board). You work closely with others. On the other hand, as an X-CORP, you have to kick your own butt into gear. There are no deadlines imposed by others when you have your own business and you won't have the project plans that keep corporate employees moving forward. *You* are the only one holding *you* accountable for your actions—or lack of action. It's not easy, so I ask again: How serious are you? Are you willing to do *whatever it will take* to build a successful small business?

How Busy Are You?

Do you often feel overwhelmed with all you have to do and the small amount of time you have to do it? If someone asks how you are, or how your business is doing, do you often reply by telling them how busy you are? This phrase is something I hear in my sleep. I hear it all the time: from my clients and the small business owners I see every day. If you're serious about building your business, then I have a request to make of you: *Stop telling everyone how busy you are.* Stop right now. Don't say it to another person. Here's why…

The Client I Never Had

When I was rebuilding my business, after our return to Florida, I felt downright overwhelmed. Not only was I servicing my existing clients, but I was building my business "by the book" and attending lots of networking meetings, plus holding a part-time job. Sometimes I'd attend meetings morning, noon and night – all on the same day. When I wasn't attending networking meetings or working with a client, I was in my office designing a new workshop. The truth is I *was* sooooo busy. Then one day at a networking meeting, I saw Phil, who owned a highly successful franchise business with about thirty employees. Phil and I had connected at past events and even met for lunch at one point. He asked how my business was doing, and I replied, "I'm sooooo busy." A number of months later, I connected with Phil yet again at a networking event. He asked me if I was still busy. I was puzzled for a moment. Phil went on to say that when he'd seen me months before, he'd wanted to ask me to come to his business and do a workshop for his employees. But . . . *I was sooooo* busy that he didn't want to bother me. Ouch.

There are two lessons here: First, watch how you "show up" with other people. If I hadn't projected to Phil that I was in "overwhelm mode," it's likely he would have hired me. I read once that either we're busy working and moving forward, or we're busy being dramatic. Which are you? We'll talk about this in Chapter Three. To discover more about yourself, answer the next question:

How Do You Spend Your Time?

As a small business owner, there's a remarkably short list of ways you should be spending your time. Checking Facebook every ten minutes isn't one of them. Neither is responding to and writing emails all day long. When you're not serving a paying client, you *must* spend your time on revenue-generating activities. Period. No excuses. Here's a little secret: Your business can grow without your being in a frenzy all the time. I'm proposing an exercise for you: For the next five business days, I'd like you to track your time. Write down everything you do between 8am and 5pm each of those days. Simply write down the activity and how much time it takes. Keep a running list. I know one thing: By virtue of the fact that you're tracking your time, you will begin to do things differently. In fact, here's something you might try:

Managing Your Email

Years ago I read about an interesting technique for handling all the phone calls and voice mails that come in during the course of the day. I've updated it for handling email. You can modify it to suit your needs, but here's an easy five-step plan to build on:

1. First thing in the morning, when you start up your computer, *do not* check your email. Take the first few minutes of every day (45 minutes works well) to plan your day and set priorities. Some business people I know prefer to do their daily planning the night before as the last thing they do before shutting down for the night. Either way works: just be sure to make it a habit, something you do every day. More than one productivity guru has called the email inbox an expansive list of priorities for everyone else—not you. "Read this." "Check this out." "What do you think of this?" They're all someone else's priorities. Make your first hour of the day productive—*for you.*

2. After setting your priorities and to-do list for the day, you can check your email inbox. Scan your inbox quickly and delete the junk. Be brutal! I find more than 60 percent of all my email is totally worthless and not deserving of the effort to click to open it. I can look down my inbox list and check off multiple messages, and then cheerfully delete them all before they get the opportunity to distract me.

3. Read and respond to the messages that need your attention. Trust me, there will only be a handful of messages that qualify.

4. After you've pruned, responded and written, *close your email program.* You may have email that arrives through a web page (i.e. Gmail, Yahoo Mail, etc.) or you may use a dedicated email program like Microsoft Outlook. No matter what it is, close it.

5. Build times into your daily schedule to check back in with your inbox. For me, I prefer once after lunch, and once again later in the afternoon, but that's just me. I do much of my work via email, so I consider it essential to check in at least twice more during the day. People who don't depend on email quite so much may be able to get away with checking only one more time during the day.

The moral of the story: Manage your email, or it will manage you.

How Willing Are You To Leave Your Comfort Zone?

Let's face it, it's more comfortable to sit in your recliner than to get up and get in the game. But *I* know that *you* know staying in your comfort zone will not result in business breakthroughs. It certainly won't result in money in the bank. In fact, it won't result in much of anything. Most of us who are X-CORPs probably thought being in our own business would be a piece of cake compared to holding down a nine-to-five job in corporate America. For most of us, however, that's not the case. I can identify with those who are terrified to attend networking meetings. I certainly was. But if you don't leave your comfort zone to get out and meet people, how will you grow your business? I sometimes go to networking meetings with my clients. I teach them how to show up, what to do, how to be comfortable and even how to have a good time. The key is to stretch yourself a little at a time. Push the boundaries of your comfort zone and there will be rewards.

Tips and Tricks to Get (Safely) Out of Your Comfort Zone

In both business and life in general, getting out of your personal comfort zone is all about gaining confidence and becoming comfortable with taking risks. After all, it's called a "comfort zone" because you're comfortable there…you know what to expect. Going out on a limb can be scary because you *might* fail. You might lose something. But a champion learns that losing isn't so bad…as long as he gets up and tries again. Here are a few -ideas you might consider trying:

> **Start slowly**: Before you make any drastic changes, try something relatively easy. You might shop at a different grocery store, sleep on the other side of the bed, or drive home using a different route. Go wild: order something from your favorite restaurant that you've never had before!

> Even trying something simple may start a noticeable increase in your stress or anxiety level. You'll feel your heart rate and breathing quicken. That's adrenaline being added to your bloodstream. In moderation, adrenaline makes you sharper, quicker, and more creative. It creates a feeling of excitement and exhilaration that comes from doing something new. Feel it…and be sure to remind yourself that it's a natural, safe reaction to trying something new. You might grow to enjoy it.

> More ideas to consider…

> **Non-attachment**: When it's time to try something new, "just do it." (Remember the old Nike tagline?) Don't worry about—or expect to get—a specific result. If you gamble, gamble with money you're ready and willing to lose; gamble for fun and the exhilaration of gambling. If you win, that's icing on the cake! But if you lose, it's no big deal. On to the next game. Let go of expecting an outcome; rather, focus on the joy of doing whatever you're doing.

> **Acceptance**: Not everything in life (or in business) will go the way you want. That's a given. When something less than perfect happens, and it will, simply shrug it off. The world

is a safe, predictable place—at least it is when you're snug as a bug in a rug in your comfort zone. But if you want to get out of that zone and move forward in leaps and bounds, you must accept both the good and the bad. You might just start thinking of that "bad" stuff as a learning experience... because it is. Life is a classroom. We can choose to learn from our experiences or not. Back in my corporate days, a mentor essentially forced me to look back on a distressing experience and figure out the lesson. My mentor instructed me I was not allowed to blame anyone—not even myself. Just thinking about it now makes my stomach churn, but it was a lesson I've carried with me for years, and I have always been extremely careful not to repeat that mistake.

Be okay with *not* knowing: When was the last time you felt excited about not knowing what was going to happen next? If you've been in that personal (or business) comfort zone for a while, you may be stuck on the idea that you have to make sure you have "all the bases covered" or have "it all figured out." See the previous note on non-attachment. Think of a first date or first kiss. Part of the excitement is in *not* knowing what might happen. Bring that feeling back into your life. It's called curiosity.

Expand your horizons: Read a book a month. Anything will do, but I suggest steering away from business topics, especially those closely related to your area of expertise. Reading a wide variety of genres will increase your vocabulary, help you better express yourself, and open your mind to new ideas and perspectives.

Connect mind and body: Find a new pastime that includes physical movement. It doesn't have to be hard work; it could be painting, dancing, learning to play a musical instrument, perfecting your voice or learning to play golf. It will be easier for you to leave your comfort zone and connect with people if you have something interesting to talk about. We all want to be around people who are energetic and engaging and, if you engage your body, not just your mind, you'll bring all of yourself into the conversation.

Speaking to new people: I love this statistic: Studies indicate that people claim their number one fear is public speaking. Number two is death. Yes, it seems that people would rather die than speak in public. But if you're in business and trying to network, speaking to new people (and maybe even to groups) will always be a crucial skill. One suggestion: Join Toastmasters.

Thus far, we've established that in order to build a successful business, it's essential to make a serious commitment, and we've also touched on the importance of maintaining a positive attitude when we talk to business associates. Remember how I lost a paying client because I moaned about how "busy" I was? In addition, we discussed why we must become comfortable *leaving* our comfort zones. Now that you're armed with the core principles to help you build the business of your dreams, let's play ball.

Winning is not a sometime thing; it's an all-time thing.
You don't win once in a while, you don't do things right once in a while...
you do them right all the time. Winning is a habit.

—Vince Lombardi

CHAPTER TWO

A REAL REFERRAL-
BASED BUSINESS
A dream come true

Referrals, referrals, referrals. That is my mantra, and it should be yours as well. Referrals can be the lifeblood of your business. Referrals *should* be the lifeblood of your business. Referrals can *double* your business.

What exactly is a referral? If you ask ten small business owners that question, you'll get ten different answers. For our purposes in this book, we'll use my definition:

> *A referral is a personal introduction to a*
> *potential client by a referral source.*

In the days before Facebook and Twitter, there were plenty of social networks and referrals going on within those networks. They were not online: Friends chatted with friends; business associates talked with business associates and compared notes, etc. Friends, and for that matter, business associates, tend to move in similar circles and go through the same experiences—not necessarily at the same time, but that doesn't matter. If I tell my neighbor that I'm thinking about getting new carpet for my home, he's going to tell me about the wonderful (or terrible) experience he had with XYZ Carpet Store.

Likewise, if I'm having lunch with a friend and mention that my business is looking for some help in the IT Department, she's likely to tell me about the experience her business had with a certain provider; she will give me a referral. It's only natural that we speak to each other in common terms and over common problems and potential solutions. We give referrals all the time, whether we know it or not.

What Makes A Great Referral

There are three components of business-building referrals: the referral source, the personal introduction, and the quality of the potential client. Let's take a look at each of these components.

The Referral Source: I've mentioned the term *referral partner* several times already. There's a difference between a referral *source* and a referral *partner*. A referral source:

- feels good about your product or service.

- understands how you can help solve the problem of a potential client.

A referral source is often—but not always, and not necessarily— someone with whom you've done business in the past. The source knows you enough to be able to refer you. While a good referral can come to you from a myriad of referral sources, your best referrals will typically come from referral *partners*. In addition to feeling good about your product or service and understanding how you can help solve the problem of a potential client, a referral partner:

- knows you and cares about what you do.

- respects you and your business.

- can describe your business well.

- understands your target market and how you serve that market.

- can set the stage for a great introduction to a referral.

- knows how to promote your business, and does.

- meets with you on a regular basis—at your invitation or theirs.

Relationships with referral partners are built over time and are beneficial to both parties. These are not accidental relationships. A referral partner will never send you on a wild goose chase. When you receive a call from a referral partner, treat that call with a sense of urgency. Arrange your calendar as necessary in order to meet with your referral partners. Referrals are the lifeblood of your business and referral partners are the lifeblood of referrals.

The Personal Introduction: The best referral is the result of a personal introduction from a referral partner, and not just a cursory, "Call this person." Decide with your referral partners how they will introduce you to a potential client. Ideally, you, your referral partner and the potential client will all meet together. Some referral partners will prefer not to be that involved. If an in-person meeting isn't feasible, suggest a three-way phone call. After all, it's the influence of your referral partner that will help you to land the business. Also, decide with your referral partners whether or not they will be involved in following up with the potential client in any way. Again, some partners will want to jump in and help you land the business; others—once they've made the introduction— will choose a hands-off approach. It's critical that you follow up with the potential client in the manner in which you agreed with your referral partner.

The Potential Client: It is up to you to educate your referral partners about your concept of the ideal client. With a *great* referral, the potential client:

- has an identified need for your product or service.

- possesses the authority to make a buying decision.

- can afford your product or service and has the ability to pay.

- is open to the possibility of working with you.

- has been educated by your referral partner on the benefits and strengths of your product or service.

- has already been "sold" on why your referral partner is bringing you together.

- is genuinely interested in a conversation with you about moving forward.

The Business That Dried Up

What are the last ten referrals you received and what are they worth? It's unfortunate, but many small business owners cannot name one. Several years ago I worked with a small business owner, Joan, who sold custom-made drapes. She had four employees and had been in business for fifteen years, but suddenly (or so she said) all her business dried up. I thought it was odd: the housing market was extremely active and Joan's target market was recent homebuyers. I asked Joan how she got her business, and she replied, "Referrals." Then I inquired about her client database. (She didn't have one.) I asked how she followed up on referrals and how she acknowledged her referral sources. (She didn't.) Ultimately, Joan had to close the doors on her business.

Create A Referral System

Don't make the same mistake as Joan. She is a perfect example of what not to do. Many savvy business people create an annual marketing plan for their businesses, or at least they have a plan to spend a certain amount each month for various forms of advertising. Yet when it comes to business-building referrals, it's much more of a "take it as it comes" system. Why leave it to chance? Create a system so you know where your referrals are coming from. You don't need to create anything fancy as long as the system works for you. My clients have used MS Outlook, MS Excel, and even a table created in MS Word. One client uses post-it notes on a bulletin board. Another uses index cards. With your system in place, take the time to track your referrals and to *acknowledge* your referral sources and partners. Keep it uncomplicated and make your system work for you and your business. If it's too complicated or too time consuming, you won't use it.

Acknowledge Your Referral Sources

Acknowledging your referral sources—recognizing and thanking them for sending business your way—is vital. Joan didn't acknowledge her referral sources, and as a result, her business dried up. Imagine if she had sent a sincere thank-you note, perhaps with a $10 Starbucks gift card, to everyone who referred a potential client to her. Joan could have held a holiday open house, which would also have been an opportunity for her to show off her lovely work. There are countless ways to acknowledge your referral sources, and we'll talk more about them in Chapter Eight. For now, suffice it to say that a "thank you" goes a long way. Nurture your referral sources and partners. Maintaining consistent and positive relationships with referral partners is a long-term investment that will benefit your business for years to come. Devote the time and effort to create powerful partnerships and both of you will see significant improvements to the bottom line.

Over the years, I slowly discovered that four foundational principles must be in place in order to build a business based on a strong referral network. I call these principles the four **A**s, and they are the basis of the A-Game of Business-Building Referrals. The four As (**A**wareness and **A**ttention, **A**uthenticity, **A**ttraction, and **A**ction) prepare you to stand above your competition, and to bring you success as you grow your business. If business were a tennis match, the four **A**s would be the grit, the power, the love and knowledge of the game. They are the core elements needed to win.

> *You've got to take the initiative and play your game.*
> *In a decisive set, confidence is the difference.*
>
> —Chris Evert

CHAPTER THREE

AWARENESS AND ATTENTION
Wake Up!

The first **A** in the A-Game is *Awareness and Attention*. Yes, I know that's two "**A**s" but they're related and connected, so read on. I suspect you've heard the adage, "sleeping on the job?" I'm sorry to say it's not unusual for me to observe small business owners who go through the motions of running a business when—in reality—that's all they're doing: Going through the motions. They don't seem to be aware of—or paying attention to—themselves and those things that are crucial for business success. Sure, they're busy, but they're often busy doing the wrong things to promote and grow their business. They always seem to be in a frenzy of activity, but is it doing any good?

Attending networking meetings without a strategy—a strategy for both the meetings and your business—is one thing I feel adds to that small business "frenzy." As I attend networking events, I usually see about half of those attending sticking to themselves, not paying attention to what's happening, and not making an effort to "network." They mechanically go through the motions of shaking hands, introducing themselves, giving out a business card, and then moving on to the next person. As a result, they miss opportunities that are all but plunked in front of them. Their bodies are present, but their brains and their hearts are not.

If you have so much on your mind that you can't be present at a networking meeting, then don't go. Here's an example of what I mean: I was chatting with a printer at a networking event. A third person, the owner of a local dry cleaning business, joined us. In the course of the conversation, the dry cleaner asked the printer how much it would cost to print one thousand flyers. The printer gave him a round number, the dry cleaner said thanks, and that was that. *The printer was half asleep!* This was a potential business opportunity, and the printer wasn't even awake enough to realize it. If the printer had been awake and aware, he could have set up a time for the dry cleaner to stop by his print shop, where he could have shown the dry cleaner his work, and asked questions so he could better understand the dry cleaner's needs. Then he could have offered the dry cleaner a proposal.

Jeff Klein, CEO of *Working for Good*, takes awareness up a notch and calls it "conscious awareness." Here's what he says: "Conscious awareness is a process of recognizing what's going on inside and out, the effects of decisions and actions, and the interaction between a complex array of factors and forces. It is seeing our seeing, observing our thoughts, and recognizing our feelings and the effect they have on us and others. Conscious awareness is a *meta skill* or *meta tool*—a skill that enhances the performance of other tools. It functions much as a mirror functions for a dancer, reflecting position and movement, providing feedback for the organism to adjust to, or as the coach in the press box serves a football team, providing a perspective on the whole field."[1] The first time I read this, I paused and then read it again. I love Klein's concept of awareness functioning as a mirror.

Awareness and Attention, the first of our four As, go hand in hand. They are the experience of mindfulness that brings expansion into focus. When you are aware, you are paying attention. You bring all your senses into the experience. When you sincerely pay attention in conversations and bring awareness of yourself and others into those conversations, your conversations will change, as will your relationships. When you pay attention, you're naturally more curious. With your curiosity awakened, your conversations will be easier and more meaningful, and your connections will turn into relationships. You may wonder when you're approached at a networking gathering how you can "wow" potential business sources. In truth, my printer colleague had all that he needed in that moment—a curious spirit, and a willingness to listen and act. Using only what he already had within, he could have landed a new customer.

As a small business owner, you must wake up. Turn up your antennae. Tune in. Teach yourself to be awake, to be aware, and to pay attention. If you run around in a half-awake state, you won't pick up on potential business that's right in front of you, just like my printer-friend. That potential business might be in the form of a phone call, something in a local business journal, a request from a potential client. But whatever it is, if your level of awareness is zero, you'll miss it. Cultivating both self-awareness and awareness of what's going on around you will allow you to more proactively and consciously build a referral business.

Self-Awareness

Self-awareness is the capacity to look objectively at ourselves: Our personality, behaviors, thought processes and motivation. It's reflecting on our strengths and our weaknesses, our habits and values. When we are self-aware, we are empowered to build on our strengths, identify areas in which we would like to make improvements and change course as necessary. In conducting research for their book, *Heart, Smarts, Guts and Luck,* authors Anthony K. Tjan and Richard J. Harrington determined that the one quality that trumps all in virtually every great entrepreneur, leader and manager is self-awareness.[2]

The two primary ways to build self-awareness are to know yourself better and become an expert self-observer. "Know yourself better" may sound silly, but trust me: Unless we've undertaken a self-study, most of us don't know ourselves that well. Personality tests such as the *DISC, Myers-Briggs, StrengthsFinder*, and others have become extremely popular. These tests facilitate self-reflection. I prefer tests that not only help you understand how you behave in certain situations, but how your behavior impacts those around you.

Self-observation is the second way to cultivate self-awareness. This involves not only being a private investigator of yourself, but doing something with the knowledge you gain. Warren Buffet, perhaps the greatest investor of all time, has mastered the skill of self-observation. I once read that he writes down his reasons for every investment he makes. Then, months later, he goes back to those reasons and learns from them. This process is called *feedback analysis*. The 2005 Harvard Business Review article, *Managing Oneself[3]*, by Peter Drucker, discusses the need to know ourselves and touts the use of feedback analysis. Athletes do this: they seek out feedback and incorporate the knowledge and advice into their style of play, so they achieve mastery over their chosen sport. (In other words, so they can play their A-Game.)

The art of building self-awareness requires that you be willing to look honestly at yourself and make changes as needed. When you become self-aware, the rewards are plentiful for your business. The exercise that follows allows you to reflect upon how you present yourself at networking events. Each time you attend a networking function, conduct your own feedback analysis by writing down the answers to these ten questions:

1. How well did I prepare for the event?

2. How did I show up (Dress, conversation, prepared with business cards, etc.)?

3. How did I talk about my business? (What words did I use?)

4. Did I stretch myself and get out of my comfort zone?

5. How did I handle myself? (Confidently, authentically, etc.)

6. Did I introduce myself to people I don't know?

7. What did I accomplish?

8. What did I learn?

9. What will I do differently next time?

10. What is my follow-up strategy? (Do I even have one?)

I suggest you purchase a notebook and write down the answers to these questions after every single meeting you attend, whether it's a networking meeting, a lunch with a referral partner, or a client meeting. Be sure to take action on your response to question number nine. Once each month, take some time to go back and read through your answers to these questions. Notice any patterns that emerge, areas for improvement, and how you can make better use of your time. Then, create a mini-action plan to address those areas in which you need to make some changes.

Building Your External Awareness Muscle

To build a referral business, you must be aware at all times of what's going on around you. Otherwise, opportunities will pass by you. Here are five ways to build your external awareness muscle:

1. Get out of the frenzy mode.

2. Admit you're not always present (and work to become more present, more often).

3. Learn to listen.

4. Perform awareness practices daily.

5. Eliminate distractions.

Get out of the frenzy mode. The number one prerequisite for raising your awareness and paying attention is to get out of the frenzy mode. Stop running around. When you create frenzy, you may feel busy and useful, but you're not paying attention to the important things. How do you do this? You practice. First, recognize that you're frenzied. Next, take a couple of deep breaths and be still. Consider what things aren't getting your attention because you are in the familiar Cuisinart of overwhelm. Then turn your attention to that important task or action. It takes practice.

Admit you're not always 100 percent present. When you're out of frenzy mode, the next step in building external awareness is simply to realize—and admit to yourself—that you're not always 100 percent present. When your mind is someplace else, you can't focus on the business at hand. Linda Stone, a thought leader, writer and consultant, coined the phrases "continuous partial attention," and "screen apnea." Continuous partial attention describes an attention strategy many of us use today. Different from simple multi-tasking (when we're often doing things that are automatic, like stirring a pot or tying a shoe) to pay continuous partial attention is to pay *partial* attention—*continuously, to more than one thing that requires cognition, like talking on the phone while writing an email.* According to Ms. Stone, this is motivated by a desire to connect and be connected. We are scanning for opportunities in any given moment and are on high alert. In small doses, continuous partial attention can be useful. Used continuously, as an attention strategy, it can put us into a state of fight or flight, causing stress, and ultimately compromising our productivity.[4] We spend a lot of time figuring out how to best manage our time. Based on Ms. Stone's research, it makes sense to spend time contemplating how we manage our attention as well. My perspective: it's okay to turn off the technology and pay attention to *people*, to make time to think and reflect, and to create opportunities for that all-powerful human connection. In fact, it's more than okay. It's mandatory for a successful business.

Learn to listen. Most of us think we're good listeners when, in reality, it takes practice to genuinely listen. To see how good a listener you are, head over to the Reader Resources page of my website at www.BusinessBuildingReferrals.com/reader-resources, and click on "Listening Assessment," then come back here. In his best-selling book, *The Seven Habits of Highly Effective People*[5], Stephen Covey said, "Seek first to understand, then to be understood." Most of us don't do this; most people do not listen at a deep level. In everyday listening, we listen mostly to the words. While the other person is speaking, we're most likely thinking about the next thing we're going to say. There's nothing wrong with listening carefully with your full attention; then when the other person is finished speaking, taking a moment or two at that time to mentally prepare a response, then speak it. Sometimes we're even more distracted: Thinking about the noises we're hearing outside, or a conversation overheard from another table in the restaurant, or even wondering what's for dinner! Next time you're in a one-on-one conversation with someone, imagine an enormous bubble around you and the other person, and then:

- Make a commitment to be 100 percent present.

- Listen with all your senses.

- Suspend all judgment.

- Listen with your ears and also your eyes.

- Be curious.

- Give 100 percent of your focus to the other person.

- Reflect back what you hear to verify your understanding.

- Ask meaningful questions.

Follow these pointers and you'll be amazed at how your listening improves, how much better you pay attention, and how much richer your conversations become.

Perform awareness practices daily. When we talk about awareness and attention in my programs, I give my participants the assignment of two daily awareness practices. These practices usually create a big "aha." In awareness practice, we become more aware of what's going on, both on the inside and the outside, by choosing where to place our thoughts. Awareness practice helps you to be present: To be here right now. Have you ever left a meeting and then noticed you couldn't recall most of what was said during that meeting? (Or am I the only one who feels that way?) The ability to turn off the churn in your mind, and to be fully awake, aware, and present will serve not only you, but those with whom you interact.

Here are the two awareness practices I assign to my A-Game program participants:

1. The timer assignment – choose a day when you plan to be at your desk for at least four hours. Set a timer for thirty minutes, and then go about your work. When the

timer goes off, stop. What are you aware of? How did you spend those thirty minutes? Did you accomplish the task or activity you had in mind for those thirty minutes? If not, what stopped or distracted you? My participants are shocked when they discover how much of their time is taken up with activities of no value.

2. The "in your car" assignment – for the next three days, each time you get in your car, turn off anything that can ring, sing or make noise of any type. This includes your radio, cell phone, iPod, etc. Enjoy the sweet silence and practice awareness:

   - What do you see while you drive?

   - What sensations do you feel in your body?

   - Are you relaxed, or tense?

   - What else?

   Some of my clients continue this practice at least two days a week because they enjoy the silence so much. Others have reported that they find themselves singing to fill the silence. Just enjoy the experience and be aware.

Eliminate distractions. The environment in which we live is intensely distracting: We're "turned on" all the time with email, mobile phones, television and radio. Regretfully, these distractions take away from our awareness and therefore, our productivity. We are lulled into a zone of unawareness. Some of my clients find themselves distracted by answering the telephone while they are working on a project. Their intention is to get a letter written. The phone rings. They answer and immediately, someone else's agenda takes over their allotted time. At the end of the day, the letter is still not written. The scene repeats the next day—and the next. Weeks later, the letter (that was supposedly critical) remains unwritten. Is it too late to write the letter? If not, guilt may take over as the letter-writing task becomes something "that would have been good to do." If the telephone is a distraction, voicemail can be your friend. Return all phone calls twice each day within an allotted timeframe. Make time commitments to yourself and keep them. It's crucial to create an environment of support for your intended tasks and actions.

Consciously building both your self-awareness and external awareness muscles will reward you in the A-Game of Business-Building Referrals.

Five Things To Be Aware Of And Pay Attention To In Your Business

You may be wondering how awareness practices will help you in business—how they'll help build your referrals and ultimately, your bottom line. Here are the five crucial parts of your business on which you can begin to focus your newfound power of attention:

1. **Why are you in business?** When I ask my clients why they went into business, they can't always answer, or at the very least, the answer is unconvincing. You must have a significant *why* to carry you through, and you must be aware of that *why* at all times. Why are you in the business you're in? As an ex-corporate person, what prompted you to go into business in the first place, and is it still a valid reason? If you're not sure why you went into business, take some time right now to reflect on this. Get in touch with what turns on your passion and fires you up.

2. **How do you spend your time?** What do you do all day long? Pay attention. "I'm sooooo busy" is a mantra I hear nearly every day. Ask yourself, "What am I busy doing and *what am I accomplishing?*" What gets done during a day? Are you engaged in revenue-generating activities or do you fool yourself into thinking you're doing what's most important? The "I'm so busy" mantra can be a way of creating a message to yourself that you're overworked and overwhelmed, so you must be doing what a successful business person does. It may also be a leftover corporate conversation. Raise your awareness of what you do all day long in your business.

3. **Who or what is your competition?** Who else does what you do? How do they do it? How do you look at your competition and how do you set yourself up for success? What do your clients spend their money on instead of spending money with you? Focus on potential clients who are in the market for the goods or services you are offering. When those people begin to shop around, what or who do they find? You need to know because this is your competition. Be aware of your competition: who they are, what they do, how they do it, and what sets you apart from them.

4. **What are your revenue and your profit?** How much revenue did you generate last year? Where is your revenue coming from? How many clients do you need to increase your revenue over the previous twelve months? What kind of client generates the most income for you? Create a plan to get more ideal clients. As a business owner, you must have a handle on the cost of doing business. Determine the activities that generate the most income, then up the ante on those activities and eliminate non-revenue generating activities. Do you keep track of the business you generate specifically through referrals? Knowing how much your business is spending on marketing and advertising overall is good, but knowing the ROI from all your different marketing campaigns is even better.

5. **Where do you get stuck?** We all get stuck sometimes. It's necessary to recognize what causes you to get stuck so you can determine how to get unstuck. There are a number of places and ways to get stuck. You may need to find help in performing a certain part of the service you offer, or in creating and delivering your product. Don't be afraid to ask for help. In corporate America, we all learned it's not okay to ask for help. It's different once you become an X-CORP. It's okay not to know everything. On the other hand, you may be getting stuck with some of the "usual suspects" of distraction: How much time do you spend on your email inbox? How much time on social media?

The partners of **A**wareness and **A**ttention are critical when it comes to creating the kind of environment that encourages and attracts your referral partners to send you referrals. Build your self-awareness muscles, cultivate awareness for what's going on externally, and pay attention to your business and you'll be on your way to building a solid referral-based business and becoming a networking super star. This may seem basic—and it is—but you'd be surprised at how many small business owners don't take these basics into consideration. Remember when Michael Jordan played basketball and as you watched him play, it was almost as though winning was somehow uncommonly basic for him? It was as though the magic came easily—naturally, from some place other than ordinary skill. Jordan always anticipated. He was keenly *aware* of himself, his teammates, and his opponents. Awareness and attention. Harness them. They're your friends, just as they were Jordan's.

> *You have to be able to center yourself,*
> *to let all of your emotions go.*
> *Don't ever forget that you play with*
> *your soul as well as your body.*
>
> — Kareem Abdul-Jabbar

CHAPTER FOUR
AUTHENTICITY
Will the real you please stand up?

Authenticity, the second A in the A-Game, has two components: *Knowing* who you are and *being* who you are. Your clients want you, not a fabulous fake. Not you pretending to be someone else. Think back on your experience in the corporate world. I'm sure you can easily remember a time with everyone sitting around a conference table nodding in agreement. It didn't matter if you agreed or not, you nodded right along, didn't you? Most likely, whatever decision was made, it was forgotten about soon after the meeting. Excuse my hard-edged honesty, but I can say from twenty-plus years of business experience: A lot of fakery goes on in the corporate world. The small business world, however, is different. As a small business owner, fakery (trying to be someone you're not) will get you nowhere—and it very well may hurt you.

Know Your Strengths

From both a business and personal point of view, it's crucial to know your strengths and weaknesses (and those of your business). In the best-selling *Strengths Finder 2.0,* author Tom Rath maintains, "All too often, our natural talents go untapped. From the cradle to the cubicle, we devote more time to fixing our shortcomings than to developing our strengths." It's exhausting to always be working on "fixing" oneself. I encourage you to discover your strengths, play to those strengths, and to find authentic ways around doing things you don't do well. Hop on over to my website (www.BusinessBuildingReferrals.com/reader-resources) for a link to the StrengthsFinder.

Remember my experience of my first-ever networking meeting—
the one I was forced to attend because a woman in the parking
lot took me by the hand? To this day, I don't love walking up
to someone at a networking meeting and introducing myself,
and it's not something at which I consider myself an expert.
However, I've found an authentic way around my discomfort:
I picture myself as the ambassador or hostess for the event;
therefore, it is my job to ensure that attendees are comfortable.
As such, it's imperative that I introduce myself to people so I
can in turn introduce them to others. When I attend networking
functions other than the Chamber of Commerce, I resolve to
find the person who seems more uncomfortable than I am. One
of my strengths is that I'm a consummate connector. So, I find an
individual who appears to be uncomfortable, introduce myself,
and offer to introduce them to others. I play to my strength of
connecting people with one another, which helps me let go of
my aversion to walking up to people and introducing myself.

Find the Person Who Is More Uncomfortable Than You Are

I had joined a club—whose members were business
professionals and community leaders—in downtown
Tampa, and I wanted to use my investment well. I had
my business cards in my jacket pocket and didn't know a
soul at a networking event. I set about to find the person
who seemed more uncomfortable than I was. I found
him holding up the door frame and looking blankly into
the room. I walked up to him and introduced myself, and
we exchanged information. He was forced to be there as
part of a job search program because he had been laid off
from a management position at a big company. I could
sense his terror: He was back on the street looking for a
job as a professional with years of experience behind him.
The future looked gloomy. I shared my lay-off experience
and invited him to be my guest at the luncheon the next
day at the same club. He accepted my invitation. Here's
the good part: We all introduced ourselves to our table
mates and when he gave his introduction, a recruiter who
sat at our table asked for his resume and said, "I have a
job for you." He was hired that quickly. That experience

always comes to mind when I am hesitant to enter into a roomful of strangers. I think that someone is in there waiting for me to introduce myself and the game is "on."

Authenticity Takes Courage

As teenagers, we didn't want to be different and stand out. Now, as a small business owner, being different and standing out—being who you truly are—will reward you. When you know yourself, when you are clear on the value you bring to your clients, when you are clear on what you can and cannot do, your clients and potential clients will take notice. This takes courage; being authentic sometimes means declining a piece of business. When we first leave the corporate world and develop our own businesses, there can be a feeling of desperation about generating revenue. We're willing to take almost any piece of business that comes our way, even if it isn't within the realm of what we offer. Don't fall into this trap. Doing something for a client that you don't do well may end up hurting your reputation. You'll stand out in the mind of a potential client if you say, "I could handle that for you, but it's not actually my forte. I'd like to refer you to Jack Jones who is a true expert at this type of project. Why don't I call him and set up a meeting for the three of us so I can introduce you to him?" Here's the bottom line: You'll quickly build trust and generate more business-building referrals from your partners as you demonstrate your honesty and integrity. Don't just suggest that a client call someone who may be able to help. Make the connection for them, take the initiative and make an honest effort to help, even if you will not directly profit from the action. Believe me, your integrity will pay you back many times over in the future.

Leave The Corporate Mentality Behind

In the corporate world, it's usually not okay to say you don't know how to do something, especially for high achievers. In my years in corporate, I observed colleagues struggling to the point of making themselves sick, often taking on more than they could comfortably or realistically handle. Many times this "Jack of all trades" mentality follows into your own business and your dealings with potential clients. You may feel it's not okay to say no, so you want to take everything that comes your way. Yet being authentic requires making choices based on your self-knowledge and having an honest view of what your business can provide. Imagine a client asking you to write their newsletter, but you're not a skilled writer. If you sign up to serve that client by writing the newsletter, you're not being authentic. The choice to go outside of your area of self-knowledge could not only be exhausting, but costly. Being authentic is not always comfortable and easy because we become stuck in our old corporate mentality, which means we continue to try to be whoever people want us to be. But as responsible business builders, we need to gather the courage to be who we are.

Lack Of Authenticity And Self-Trust (The Signs)

When we feel people are authentic, we trust them. In his book, *The Speed of Trust*, best-selling author Stephen Covey poses the question, "If you can't trust yourself, how can you expect others to trust you?" In that same vein, if you don't feel authentic, how can you expect others to see you as such? Here are nine signals that you may be losing trust in yourself, and that personal authenticity may be evading you:

1. Feelings of anxiety – you may be trying to "show up" in a way that isn't really you.

2. Trying to please others in ways that go against your values, your beliefs, or strengths.

3. Rationalizing – "I'll do this and he'll never know."

4. Trying to look good and impress others – exaggerating your accomplishments will get you nowhere. People will see right through you.

5. Saying or doing things you regret – "Oh yeah, I can do that!" Then wondering, "What in the world did I sign up for?"

6. Hiding or denying your feelings – ignoring your intuition and that little voice inside your head.

7. Feeling victimized – "I have to do this because…"

8. Feeling paralyzed or helpless – because you're unwilling to admit that you don't know.

9. Getting trapped – you bit off more than you can chew, but don't want to admit it.

Provide Value…and Be Valued

A former client of mine, a computer technician, whom I'll call Joe, came to me because he was struggling in his business. As a former corporate employee, Joe had that corporate mentality of "If I stay late, my boss will think I'm doing a great job." That type of thinking indicates a lack of self-trust, but that was Joe's mindset. In keeping with that mindset, Joe gave away—in other words, he didn't charge for—extra work for his clients. He would be hired to "get rid of a virus" and would spend a day at a client's office doing much more than he had originally agreed to do. In the course of conversation, his clients would mention that they needed this and that fixed, too, and since he was already there, couldn't he fix it?

Joe always did the extra work, but he didn't charge for it. He never told his clients this. After a couple of meetings, Joe and I were able to determine that he wanted his clients to think he was terrific, in much the same way that he wanted his former corporate boss to think he was terrific, so he was providing valuable services to his clients for free. I also learned that Joe didn't even tell his clients that the extra work was complimentary, so he wasn't getting recognition from his customers for going the extra mile. Joe didn't trust himself. Was giving away the store, so to speak, the right and authentic thing to do for his business? Joe thought people would see him as magnanimous, but when he didn't tell them he was including the extra work for free, there was no benefit. It was all based on his old desire to be seen as a good guy, a typical achievement behavior associated with going above and beyond.

How To Increase Self-Trust And Authenticity

As an X-CORP, are you at all like Joe with a leftover corporate "disease to please?" How many times have you made an agreement with yourself that you didn't keep? If I had a dollar for all the times I told myself I'd get up the next morning and walk for two miles, I'd be a wealthy woman. There was a time when I would give away time I'd scheduled for myself on my calendar. I'd give that time to whoever wanted it: a client, a friend, my family. All those times I didn't get up and go for that walk and all those times I gave away time on my calendar were messages that I couldn't trust myself. Then one day I realized that, if I couldn't trust myself, how could I expect my clients to trust me? Now when I put time on the calendar for myself, I keep those commitments. I've found that if clients start cancelling their appointments with me, it's an indicator that I might not be keeping my commitments to myself and my business.

The conversations we have with ourselves are vital. Ask yourself, "Is the way I talk with myself and about myself authentic? Am I telling myself the truth?" Here are seven ways to increase self-trust and your authentic self:

1. Identify your fears and get clear about them. You may not be able to "fix" them all, at least not immediately; but if you're aware of fears and limitations, you'll be better able to work around them as they come up on a day-to-day basis.

2. Increase the volume of your intuition and listen to it.

3. Celebrate your successes and take note of the strengths behind those successes.

4. Determine where you struggle and why.

5. Find ways to enjoy the moment. Be present in the here and now.

6. Observe the ways in which you get yourself into overwhelm. If you know the signs that signal the start of your "frenzy," you may be able to nip it in the bud.

7. Love who you are.

Be authentic about who you are and the value you bring. Be willing to tell the truth. Be willing to stand up for who you are.

Authenticity = Attraction

As you go through your day, focus on being a client-attracting "magnet." Believe—and **know**— that you are putting out "good vibes" that will attract new clients and business to you. You don't have to make a distinct effort of any kind to be "magnetic," just begin to develop the mindset that people will be happy to meet you and to learn about your business and what it can do for them. I'm sure you've met and know people who seem to draw others to them with a powerful magnetic force. It's a type of charisma, to be sure, but it's not all about the personality. Those magnetic folks aren't necessarily loud or self-promoting. They have a quality of likeability and personal integrity that just seems to draw other people to them in an easy, natural way. You are your own best referral source. When you're authentic, people are attracted to you. To learn more about attraction, read on.

I have always tried to be true to myself,
to pick those battles I felt were important.
My ultimate responsibility is to myself.
I could never be anything else.

—Arthur Ashe

CHAPTER FIVE
ATTRACTION
Become a client magnet

Attraction is the third foundational principle in the A-Game. You may have heard of the *Law of Attraction,* introduced to the mainstream a few years ago by the popular video, *The Secret.* The Law of Attraction essentially states that—good or bad, wanted or unwanted—*what you focus on is what you get.* As far as our discussion of referral-based business is concerned, Attraction is one of the foundational principles of the A-Game. It's a basic element and indispensable building block when it comes to creating a successful and enjoyable business. As we tune into our true desires (Awareness), and become clearer about who we are (Authenticity), we increase our powers of Attraction. The idea is to become a powerful magnet for our referral partners and ultimately, our ideal clients.

The Attraction Factor

Think about service providers and sales people you deal with on a regular basis or have dealt with in the past. What attracts you to these individuals and/or their companies? I recently had this discussion with a client of mine, Debbie. I asked her to think about the last person she hired for anything. It was a personal trainer she'd hired about two months prior. Debbie is one of those women who's been in terrific shape her entire life. Then, a couple of years ago, she injured her back and ended up with a herniated disc. It took months for her back to heal. When it was time for her to get back to working out, she kept finding excuses. She was both surprised and disappointed in herself and finally decided she needed to hire a personal trainer. What's the first thing she did? She spoke to a friend and neighbor, who sang the praises of her own personal trainer. A referral was born!

Debbie called the trainer who immediately offered her a half hour of his time to meet, visit the workout facility and answer any questions she might have. At that initial meeting, she committed to working with him for a minimum of three months. Debbie and I reflected on the "attraction factors" from that initial meeting with the trainer:

- He was positive, upbeat and smiled a lot.

- He had an advanced degree in exercise physiology.

- He worked primarily with baby boomers and those who have had injuries.

- He was very up front in telling her they would need to start slowly.

- He was willing to make a change in his schedule so she could meet him at 7:30 in the morning.

- He extended to her the "summer discount" since she was referred by her neighbor who was already a client.

As of this writing, Debbie has had weekly workouts with this trainer for four months. Not only are those same attraction factors still at work, but now there are a few more:

- If his next client has cancelled, the trainer is always happy to offer Debbie a few extra minutes at no charge, but he always asks her first instead of assuming she has the time.

- She feels he over-delivers and provides more than the value she's paying for.

- She fully trusts he has her best interests at heart.

- He seems genuinely interested in her as a person, not just as a client.

What attracts you to those with whom you do business? This would be a perfect time to take out a pen and notebook, and make a few notes before reading on.

Define Your Ideal Client

If the goal is to become a client magnet, and what you focus on is what you get, then it's crucial to define your ideal client so you can begin to put the attraction factor to work. An understanding of your ideal client is an asset when you look for referral partners: A clear definition of your ideal client's profile will make it much easier to find and build relationships with referral partners. You'll also be prepared when a referral partner asks, "Who are your best clients?" You need to be able to answer with conviction. When you worked in the corporate world, defining your target market and ideal client was probably something left to a separate department (unless you worked in the Marketing department). But now, as an X-CORP, it's entirely up to you to determine the clients who are right for your business, your service, and your products.

Clients are the lifeblood of any business, and we all want more of them. When I first started my business, I wanted—and would take—any client I could get my hands on. I had no idea there could be "right" clients and "wrong" clients. I just wanted clients who would pay me. Now that I have the experience and wisdom to look back, I can see I was the one who ended up paying the price in dealing with clients who were not a good fit for me. When you work with those who are not your ideal clients, it can be a struggle. You work way too hard and often earn less or you feel you're not being paid fairly for the work you're doing. Getting clear on your ideal client (remember: **A**wareness) isn't something that would be *nice* to do. It's not a luxury. It's a mandate. Working with only "ideal clients" results in a better bottom line, not to mention vast improvements in your personal sense of satisfaction.

For starters, here are seven criteria to use when determining your target market. Your ideal client:

- is someone who has a need for the products and/or services you have to offer.

- has the money to pay you.

- sees value in what you have to offer and respects the work you do.

- will refer you to others without being asked.

- comes back to you for more of whatever it is you offer.

- shares your core values.

- energizes you.

These criteria apply, no matter what your business is. With these "generic" rules in mind, you can further refine your list. It's time to take out your notebook and pen again. Here are some questions to help you hone in on the specifics of your ideal client:

- What expertise do you bring from the corporate world, and who are the potential clients who can relate to you and your expertise?

- What clients have you most enjoyed working with in the past? What attributes do they share?

- Who (or what type of business) benefits most from working with you?

- What demographics do your clients have in common? (Age, gender, income, location, etc.)

If you haven't done so yet, take as much time as you need to go through the exercise above and define your "ideal client." This is important for a number of reasons, but it's especially important when it comes to attracting clients and referral partners to you and your business.

Putting Attraction To Work For Your Business-Building Referrals

As a small business owner, it's essential to remember that opportunities for marketing happen all the time, each and every day. Your loved ones probably aren't going to become clients anytime soon, but all other people could be potential clients. Whenever you're around people, you should be prepared to seize the opportunity to share your business story, to allow your integrity and honesty to shine through, and to make new friends and meet potential clients. It's an old cliché, but it's true: You are a walking billboard for your business and, as such, when you speak and interact with others, you're engaged in a potential marketing experience. Remember: you are marketing yourself—and, in turn, your business—all the time, whether you're actively aware of that fact or not. So stay on your toes and make good, conscious decisions about the messages you're relaying to others. It doesn't matter how those messages are being transmitted: in person, over the phone, through a Facebook or Twitter post, or even while ordering lunch at the local deli. Almost everything you do is a marketing opportunity, and each interaction you have should be viewed as a chance to build a connection with someone.

Just as muscles can be built, so can our powers of connection, attraction and influence. We connect because attraction draws us together. Attraction can be used to bring people and material things together for the greater good, and that "bringing together" is the result of a good referral system. It pushes us past resistance, or separation, and helps us X-CORP folks develop our influence muscles. Creating and developing the skills of attraction is an art, not a science; there's no formula or exact recipe to follow. You must develop your own method, and follow your own intelligence and intuition.

Ten Ways To Build Your Attractor Muscles

1. Make some kind of strategic marketing outreach with your current clients. Aim for a simple goal such as getting your clients to take some sort of action: "Like"

your Facebook page, download a coupon, come in to your location for a special deal, anything at all. Just get clients into the habit of taking action when you ask them to.

2. Change something: your in-store displays, your website, your offline advertising. People ignore what looks the same or seems old and stale.

3. Visit your clients' Facebook pages and "like" them and their businesses. Use Twitter or other social media outlets to increase your visibility.

4. Sign up for a class to learn something new, then share the learning experience with your clients.

5. Invest in yourself. When is the last time you read a good book, took a class or attended a powerful seminar?

6. Schedule one-on-one conversations with your employees (if you have them) or with ten of your clients. Keep it casual. Ask questions. You'll be amazed at what you learn.

7. Suggest cross-marketing to a small business owner with whom you can partner. Brainstorm ways to generate more business by working together.

8. Network with influential members of your community.

9. Get involved in new community initiatives that could impact your business.

10. Host a brainstorming session with other businesses to explore how you can collaborate to increase each other's business.

Here's another super-simple, super-powerful idea: Start paying more attention to the conversations around you. You'll probably notice that most conversations are complaints, negative exchanges or gossip. There isn't much that's uplifting and supportive. Why do we complain so much? That old saying is probably true: Misery loves company. How do you feel after being a part of conversations like that? I know I come away from most of those conversations feeling exhausted and dispirited. People say they don't want negativity in their lives, and yet they still take part in negative-energy conversations, which only gives the negativity even *more* energy. Remember, what you focus on is what you get, whether it's positive or negative. And if we're engaged in negative thinking or conversations, we may be attracting exactly what we don't want. So here's some advice: Give up the negative conversations. Pay attention to your words and language. Break out of the habits that keep you from experiencing what you honestly want. Some people refuse to read the newspaper or watch the news because the media often focuses on unpleasant content that makes them miserable. Some business owners forbid negative conversations in their places of business. Whatever course you take, it's important to become aware of your actions and the things you do that invite negative forces into your life—and then to determine how you're going to eliminate them and work on your "attraction muscles" instead.

You may have to make some changes—possibly big changes—in your personal and business life to build those "attraction muscles." (If you're content with the level of business you currently have, there's no need to read further.) Still with me? Good! If you want to bring your dreams to life, then you may need to step out of your current circle or network. Find a group with connections that will draw you out of your comfort zone. I've already told you how difficult it is for me to step outside of my own comfort zone. At one point, I knew I needed to step it up and step out, so I accepted an invitation to attend an event for a candidate who was running for political office. I don't consider myself a "political animal," and it was all somewhat strange and new to me. In fact, I felt pretty out of place, a stranger in a strange land, if you will, so I familiarized myself with her platform and her views on various issues. By the time the event was held, I was excited, eager and genuinely interested. I met many new people and actually listened to the conversations. Attending that one event inspired me to become more involved in my local community, and now it's something I relish. I'm still a work in progress, but I pushed myself and it's paying off.

Reaching loftier goals requires bringing your A-Game and often being willing to play against bigger players on a much larger field. You'll have to make some pretty hardcore decisions about what's right for you and your business, growth-wise; but I can assure you: You can't win against a stronger team unless you have players who are willing to go out on that field and fight. And the key to their success is a strong coach, a person who plans in advance, studies the whole picture and thinks big. Without a savvy leader, it'll be pretty tough to achieve your goals, no matter how hard you fight. It really is that simple, which is why I encourage you to find a coach or accountability partner of your own to assist you in this new "game."

Look at the people around you: your friends and business associates. Are they challenging themselves to play a bigger game? Or are they content just to play a lazy game? Personal development gurus have a saying: Take a look at the five people closest to you, and you'll know your own level of success. Those five influence you in so many ways, so be sure those people are supportive, uplifting and inspiring you to play your best game. You may need to make some changes in that inner circle: Surround yourself with winners so that you also will be a winner.

Whether or not you believe in the attraction element, you can't deny the fact that when you focus on pessimistic thoughts, negative actions usually occur. For example, if you dwell on the fact that you have no money, you're probably going to remain broke. If you concentrate on the number of "bad" clients you have, more than likely, you'll end up with more of the same. However, if you focus on generating more referrals from your referral partners and shifting your thoughts to positive, proactive actions, what usually happens? You may not become an overnight success, but you've taken steps in the right direction.

The human brain is an amazing, unique organ that not only acts like a supercomputer but likes being busy. It specializes in higher-level problem solving skills and creativity, so it shouldn't be too difficult for you to put that brainpower to work and determine a way to expand your referral-based business. Right? Since you've got complex abilities, you might as well put them to good use. After all, it makes really good business sense, and your ideas might amaze you.

There is no "magic" in the power of attraction, but you can make the power of attraction work for you in magical ways. All it takes is a good business plan. The clearer the plan, the more easily you'll attract the success you seek. Don't make excuses for yourself. Each time you rationalize a behavior by saying, "I can't do this" or "I don't want to do this," stop, take a deep breath, rethink your position and don't let yourself fall back into that trap. People who use too many excuses to avoid action are setting themselves up for failure. And failure definitely is not what you're working toward. Excuses –whether you voice them or not – create negative, self-defeating actions. But positive statements like, "I can do this" or "I'll give it a try," create positivity. If you want to be an attraction magnet, it's important to believe in your powers of attraction and engage in activities that have a positive impact on you and your business.

Attracting the best people and situations isn't difficult. Keep in mind that your available network (people, experiences and situations) is a lot bigger than you probably realize. Think about who could use your help and make a note of how you might help or serve certain people. This is a great exercise. It expands your thinking and opens you to infinite possibilities. I'm always astounded when I do this activity because amazing things occur: I run into people I've listed and, oftentimes, I'm able to serve them. Although my interactions might not result in revenue, it certainly builds more solid relationships and connections. It's also exciting to me to know that I'm able to help others with my knowledge, experience or suggestions. Sharing your expertise with others creates positive communication, renewed energy and mutual respect. Even without immediate financial reward, you can trust that you'll receive payback at some point in the future. That's the way our Universe works.

I'm often amazed when many small business owners are reluctant to express what they want. When asked, they may respond with vague answers, but it's no secret that most business owners have pretty good ideas about the directions in which they'd like to see their businesses grow: They're just too afraid to voice them. Unfortunately, many people equate failure to achieve a goal with the feeling that they were "wrong" to have wanted something in the first place—and that's a shame. When people base their self-worth on whether or not they achieve certain goals, the impact can be discouraging. Very few business owners can attain every goal, but creating an intention, a plan, and then moving towards the goals listed in the plan will help you move forward to success. Always bring your best attitude and best abilities— your A-Game. Don't "grade" yourself, and don't let those excuses we talked about earlier stand in your way. You simply need to set your sights higher for your business if you want to establish a referral-based business. Michael Jordan once said, "I've missed more than 9,000 shots in my career. I've lost almost 300 games. Twenty-six times, I've been trusted to take the game winning shot and missed. I've failed over and over and over again in my life. And that is why I succeed." It doesn't get much more basic than this.

The first thing is to love your sport.
Never do it to please someone else.
It has to be yours.

—Peggy Flemming

CHAPTER SIX
ACTION IS THE ANSWER
Get off the couch and get in the game

Action is the fourth A in the A-Game. To get results, you must take action. Period. If you're not getting the results you want in life, especially in building your referral-based business, then take a look at your actions—or inaction. Motivational speaker and self-help author Tony Robbins says, "A real decision is measured by the fact that you've taken a new action. If there's no action, you haven't truly decided." I know I've said this before, but it's serious enough to repeat in different ways: every day I come in contact with small business owners who don't feel productive. The reason for this feeling is simple: It's because they're *not* productive. They're spinning their wheels. They sit and stare at the computer, fooling themselves into thinking they're working. They allow themselves to be mesmerized by their email or by reading their friends' latest Facebook posts. (Is it important to know what your friends had for lunch today?) When they do take action, they take the *wrong* action.

It's been my experience and observation that small business owners often get into the habit of taking the wrong actions on a daily basis. Eventually, they get to the point where they don't know the difference between how they *should* be spending their time and how they *should not* be spending their time. As a former corporate employee, you know all about performance reviews. Corporate employees get measured on the results they've achieved as a result of the action they've taken during a specific time frame. If you had to give yourself a performance review right now—as CEO of your business—how would you fare? Would you give yourself a raise? Would you fire yourself?

Action Versus Intention

Thinking about doing something and actually doing it are two *decidedly* different things. Don't fool yourself into thinking you're in action just because you have some *ideas* about what to do. It may feel like you're in action because you've given so much thought energy to what you want to do. You plan to plan, but never get into real action. *Nothing happens until you take action and create momentum.* Remember: Action requires traction, not distraction. One of the assignments I give my program participants is to name a potential referral partner, do some research on that person, and then take action. Participants are always eager to get into action conducting their research, but they often get stuck there: They do their research, do more research, and then even more research. "Doing research" sometimes becomes an excuse for not taking the next step: making contact. They *intend* to make contact. After all, they're doing all this research.

The solution is simple: You must create rock-solid schedules and deadlines around your actions. All of your actions must have dates that specify when you will start and when you will finish. As you create your list of goals and intentions for any business-related project, don't just write a to-do list. Make sure you create a "completion date" for each project. There are many books on planning and scheduling. Find one that works for you and put it into action.

Goal Planning And Implementation

Goals are the catalyst for action. A clearly defined set of your top ten goals for the year—that you work on every day—will get you into action and keep you there. Every small business owner should use some sort of goal planning and implementation process to keep themselves on track. It can be a system you create yourself, or one of the many systems available online. A goal is a desired outcome. How does one achieve a desired outcome? By taking action. First, determine what you want to achieve. Next, decide on the appropriate action. Then, take action. For more information on goal planning and implementation, please visit my website, www.BusinessBuildingReferrals.com/reader-resources.

Avoidance

Some small business owners fall into the avoidance trap, often without realizing it. What do I mean by "avoidance?" Simple: You're busy. You do a lot of things during the day, but you're avoiding doing the valuable stuff, the actions that move the business forward. If you're not getting the results you want, but you know you've been in action, then it's time to take a good hard look at the actions you've taken and ask yourself, "Am I doing one thing to avoid doing another?" Sometimes the answer to this question isn't quite clear. If it's not, then ask yourself, "If I *were* avoiding something, what would it be?" The answer to this question can be very telling.

Avoidance Will Get You Nowhere

My client, Susan, designed her brochure. Then she redesigned it. Then she designed it again. She insisted her business cards be perfect and spent an inordinate amount of time designing them. Then she redesigned them. She wasn't taking any action. When her brochure and her business cards were finally in her hands, she made a commitment to attend a Chamber of Commerce networking event. We worked together to get her prepared: how she would dress, how she would introduce herself, what she would say about her business. She was prepared, albeit hesitant. The event began at 7pm. At 7:15pm I called her home. She answered. She had decided not to go to the event. The designing and redesigning of business cards and brochures was an avoidance tactic. In the end, Susan gave up the idea of her own business and re-entered the job market.

You must get off the couch and get in the game. Take action, or nothing happens.

What Motivates You To Take Action?

There are reasons behind our actions and various psychological theories explaining those reasons. One such theory is the Achievement Motivation Theory developed by David McClelland, PhD.[6] His needs-based motivational model has been used in corporate America for years. You may even be familiar with it. Dr. McClelland's theory indicates that all workers are driven to varying degrees by three social motives: Achievement, Affiliation and Power. This mix of motivational needs is what makes us do what we do in the work environment. I maintain that these motivators carry over and get played out as we move from being corporate employees to small business owners. Let's take a look at these needs, and how they might be impacting the action you take:

Achievement – those driven by this motivator have a need for the attainment of realistic but challenging goals, and advancement on the job. There is also a strong need for feedback about achievement and progress, and a need for a sense of accomplishment. Many of us who came from a corporate environment are driven by an innate need to achieve. In the corporate world, however, our goals were often set for us. If we wanted to stay employed, if we wanted a pay increase, we strived to achieve those goals. Corporate high achievers bring that same need to their work as small business owners. What motivates you? For a lot of X-CORPs, I find the main driving force is achievement. It's only natural. In the corporate environment, most are surrounded by other high achievers, and they're all in performance-based compensation and promotion systems. Healthy corporations support those efforts with things like performance reviews and management acknowledgement, not to mention increases in salary and benefits. For many small business owners, there's a sense of isolation in working on their own. Their drive for achievement does not come with the same recognition that it did in the corporate environment. There's no pat on the back from management, no recognition from co-workers. Sometimes it seems to me that all that networking frenzy (going to networking meetings and striving to meet as many people as possible) stems from the desire to be back on a team, to be part of a collaborative effort. When I ask my clients for a strategic plan to underpin their networking efforts, their eyes glaze over. The answer is usually, "I have no idea." For many X-CORPs, networking is satisfying another need altogether: the need to be in the company of other high achievers. There's nothing wrong with that. It's just not the way to build a solid referral business.

Affiliation – those driven by affiliation have a need for friendly relationships and interaction with other people. They also have a need to feel liked and popular. In a corporate environment, there's a lot of affiliation going on: Attending staff meetings, partnering on projects, meetings with your boss and/or meetings with those who report to you. As a small business owner, we often feel alone. Attending lots of networking meetings can become a substitute for your old staff meeting. A recent client, an X-CORP, read all the books and attended every networking meeting imaginable. I questioned the amount of time, effort and money he spent attending several networking meetings each week and so we conducted an analysis: We looked at each of his networking activities and calculated his return on investment of time, energy, effort, money and emotion. His ROI at one particular weekly networking meeting became crystal clear: It gave him zero return, *and* it cost him a lot in terms of time, energy, effort and money. When I suggested he give up his membership in that group, he declared, "But those are my friends!" It didn't take long for me to realize that his attendance at networking events was not about business-building; rather it was to satisfy a need for social interaction. Eventually, I fired him as a client. I could see that refusing to pare down his networking meetings to two per week (from ten!) would stand in the way of any business coaching I might provide. His business could easily have generated a six-figure income if he had paid more much-needed attention to his potential and current clients. I later learned that he closed the doors to his business just three months after our last meeting. Let's be clear: There's nothing wrong with making friends with the people you meet at networking events. However, if your sole purpose in attending the event is to socialize and "be with your buddies," then admit that you're not networking to build new relationships and ultimately, you will not build your referral business.

Power – those who are motivated by power have a need to be influential, effective and to make an impact. There is a strong need to lead and for their ideas to prevail, as well as a need to increase personal status and prestige. The power motive is the one that the successful small business owner must exercise. The motive is like a muscle: The more you work it, the more powerful it becomes. Influence and power are the ability to impact others positively by connecting with them physically, emotionally and intellectually. In other words, people will like you even if they hardly know you. They are drawn to you. This personal magnetism sets you apart from the rest of the crowd. Here are four ways to demonstrate power:

- You inspire people. Your energy and passion are contagious.

- You have the ability to cut through the details and get to the heart of the matter.

- You are a natural listener.

- You love new information and know instinctively how to use it effectively for the benefit of others.

The truth is we are all able to improve our "influence skills" to become... more influential!

One of the benefits of corporate life was that it satisfied our deep desire to achieve—and to receive praise and reward for our achievements. Our former roles came with automatic affiliation. There was no question. We belonged to a group, and there was a measure of comfort, security, and fellowship with our cohorts. Yet there is a paradigm shift (from super achiever to super influencer)

that must occur if we are to grow as small business owners and that shift makes all the difference in growing a referral business.

Action Exercises

To build a referral business, you must take action. The right action. Here are two exercises that will help you create your own successful daily action plan:

The daily list: As you go through your day, make a list of everything you do. Simply jot down each activity or action as you do it: Email, reading the local Business Journal, working on a client project, coffee with a colleague, surfing the Internet, writing a blog post, posting on Facebook, etc. Then at the end of your day, go back to your list and write down the result—or payoff—of each action. You will undoubtedly discover that you stay busy doing a lot of things that have no payback. These things take up chunks of time in your day, but yield no result. I have a good friend, a realtor, who always has a long   to-do list. Yet a close inspection of the list shows none of those actions or tasks actually supports revenue generation. It is certainly possible—but highly unlikely—that posting on Facebook is a well-considered strategy to build your system of influence. Again, it may be for your business, and I don't want to discourage you if it honestly is. But please, be honest with yourself. If you are posting on Facebook just because, then this is an opportunity to rethink and adjust your activities in support of revenue generation.

The "unbusy" exercise: With your daily list in hand, commit (for one day) to stop doing all those things you discovered that keep you busy, but produce no results. Spend an entire day being "unbusy." When my program participants do this exercise, they eliminate things like email, Facebook, Twitter, watching videos on YouTube or the Home Shopping Network on television, and talking on the phone with friends. Go about your normal workday, but without the busy activities. At the end of your day, ask yourself if you've produced anything of value... done anything that supports marketing, client contact, revenue generation, etc. Most small business owners who do this find that they want to continue selecting one day out of the work week to put the brakes on busy work and devote the day to more reflective or planning-oriented activities.

✳

You must take action. *Thinking* about taking action is like having your foot on the brake and gas at the same time: You go nowhere. The daily list and the "unbusy" exercise will help you to discover just how you're spending your time and if you're taking the right action. Here are four questions I find useful when it comes to Action:

- What action can I take now that will have the biggest impact on my business?

- What impact will this action have?

- What obstacle is in the way of my taking this action?

- How can I move this obstacle out of my way?

When you play the A-Game, you need to score if you're going to win.

The Job's Not Finished Until The Celebration Is Over

As you create and follow your plans to get into action—and carry out those actions—there's one step that many small business owners and managers often overlook. You've set the goals, you've made the plans and have gotten everything done within the schedules and deadlines you've created. Wonderful! Now it's time to celebrate your success. You don't need to have an office party each time some small step is completed, but it's essential to recognize and celebrate small successes as they happen. Small successes strung together over time lead to the major, breakthrough accomplishments that create successful businesses.

As a small business owner and operator, you may be the only "staff" in your company. You may want to share your successes with family and friends, and bring them in on recognizing and celebrating accomplishments. There's never a bad reason to take a spouse or loved one out to dinner for a little celebration, right? Also, including family and friends in the celebration only adds to the motivational powers of the entire process. Those around you will be even more supportive and encouraging, when they know what you're up to, and appreciate your struggles and successes. Motivational experts always recommend telling family and friends when you're making (or trying to make) significant life changes such as losing weight or quitting smoking. Once your friends have a better understanding of your business, they'll be more likely to offer support and help each step of the way.

The same applies to celebrating business success. As your "inner circle" learns of your successes, they'll encourage you on to bigger and better things. One last thought about celebrations: Don't wait for some special day or event to celebrate. Don't wait for the end of the month or even the end of the week (unless your success falls on those days). Celebrate the small victories, and they'll lead to the bigger and bigger successes. The immediate feedback to yourself and those around you will be much more powerful and motivating when you celebrate "as it happens."

With four **A**s under your belt, you will be prepared to rise above your competition, to choose your referral partners and grow your business. The game is just beginning. Are you ready to play?

No excuses. No explanations.
You don't win on emotion.
You win on execution.

—Tony Dungy

CHAPTER SEVEN

BUILD YOUR NETWORK
The A-Game way

Most X-CORPs do what they're told because that's the way to be successful in the corporate world. When they go out on their own, these X-CORPs continue to do what they're told: They read all the books about how to build a business and then do what the guru-authors tell them to do: Run around to every networking event possible. You must do this (so say the gurus) because you don't have a hefty marketing budget.

Is this the way you've been trying to build your business? Have you been attending networking meetings morning, noon and night? If so, in the words of Dr. Phil, "How's that working for you?" My guess is that it's probably not. It never worked for me, and it doesn't work for my clients. You don't see CEOs of companies running around to networking events to build their businesses. Instead, they strategically build alliances with individuals and companies with whom they can do business: individuals and companies they can help, and who can help them. *They build a network,* and that's what building your network the A-Game way is all about: Thoughtfully and strategically building a set of connections (people and companies) whom you can help, and who can help you. There's reciprocity in the formula. It's not all about you. It's about what you and your alliances can create together. How do you find these alliances? You start networking.

Dictionary.com defines networking as "a supportive system of sharing information and services among individuals and groups having a common interest."[7] I agree with this definition only to a point. For our purposes, here's the definition we'll use:

*Networking is making a connection and then
creating and nurturing a relationship from that connection.*

We have so many ways of making contact in today's world: social media, email, smart phones, Skype, Facebook, etc. While these various means of making contact are helpful, they fall short: There's a difference—a big difference—in sending or receiving an email versus actually reaching out and touching someone in person. A warm handshake, eye to eye contact, and the dance of human interaction provide an emotional connection that can't be made over the Internet or on the telephone. The most effective networking includes face-to-face contact. Networking happens between two people. It's not a team sport. When done properly and with that Law of Attraction "intention" we've discussed, networking is the way to build your A-Game network.

As a former corporate employee, you may have done networking in your previous position, though you may not have thought of it as networking. You may have attended key meetings, trade shows, seminars and other events where you participated in similar types of networking activities. But it's also possible that—again, depending on your position—you may have had no reason for true networking out there in the "real world." But now, as a small business owner, networking becomes a vital skill in creating success for your business. To get the best return possible on the investment of time, energy, emotion, effort and money you put into your networking, and in order to build your network (to become a networking super star), you must arm yourself with answers to the following questions:

- What's unique about you?

- What's the value you bring to your clients?

- What are the right words to use when talking about your business?

- What's your elevator pitch?

- How do others—including your clients—talk about you and your business?

- How can you help others talk about your business?

- How do you want to show up?

- How do others perceive you?

Let's take a look at each of the above questions.

What's Special And Unique About You?

When I ask new clients or program participants what's unique about them, more often than not, the response is vague and uninteresting: "I provide great customer service," or "I'm honest." To this, I say, "So what?" As a business owner, it's expected that you are honest and that you provide excellent customer service. Honestly, there's nothing remarkable about those two attributes. Until and unless you can talk about what makes you stand out from your competition, and why a potential client should be excited to do business with you, attracting new business will be a challenge.

It's not always easy to put your arms around the answers to these questions. In fact, it's such a challenge that some X-CORPs don't even bother. Recently I was at a networking meeting in which each participant had a chance to introduce themselves. A realtor stood up and said, "My name is Jackie. I'm a realtor. You know what I do." I was dumbfounded. Would you want to do business with a realtor—or any businessperson, for that matter—who shows no excitement about her work? I wouldn't. I happen to know that Jackie specializes in working with first-time home buyers. She could have said, "Hi, I'm Jackie. I'm a realtor who specializes in helping my clients find their first dream home." Wouldn't that have been much better?

How To Figure Out What's Unique About You

By now I hope you understand how beneficial it is for you to spend time determining your uniqueness. If *you* don't know who you are, how can you tell other people? You've probably heard the term "USP," which stands for "Unique Selling Proposition," and that's precisely what we've been talking about. To determine your USP, start by asking yourself a few questions:

- Who are the clients that benefit most from my product or service?

- What do I love most about my work?

- What do I do best?

- What seems to get rave reviews from my clients?

Follow up your answer to each of these questions by asking yourself, "So what?" As you drill down on each of these questions, you'll discover your uniqueness.

When I asked a recent client of mine what was unique about him, he didn't know. He's a building contractor, and his thinking was that there's nothing unique about the contracting business. When I asked him what got rave reviews from his customers, he told me his customers love the fact that he personally visits each and every work site every day to inspect the work being done by his subcontractors. If the work isn't done properly, it gets torn out and redone. His subcontractors know that he may show up at any time, and as a result, they never try to cut corners and usually the work is done right the first time. If you've ever built a home or been through a renovation, then you know how unusual this is. This client's USP became "the contractor who is fussier about your new home than you are." Here are a few more winning examples of USPs:

A copywriter: "Compelling copy guaranteed to get your phone to ring…or your money back."

Jewelry designer: "Necklaces that make you stand out in a crowd."

SEO expert: "Your number of website visitors will double in sixty days. Guaranteed."

For more help on your USP, please visit my website, www.BusinessBuildingReferrals.com/reader-resources.

How Do You Talk About Your Business?
(Your Elevator Pitch)

I will never forget how one particular gentleman introduced himself to me at a Chamber of Commerce function a couple of years ago: "You know what insurance is. That's what I do. When you need insurance, come and talk to me." I can assure you, he isn't generating much enthusiasm with that pitch. Do you talk about your business in a way that shows you love what you do? Do you smile and talk about your business with passion? Does your face light up? The way you talk about your business influences how others will talk about your business. In fact, the way you talk about your business *teaches* others how to talk about your business. Taking the time to figure out how to introduce yourself and how to talk about your business will reward you a thousand times over.

You may have heard the terms *elevator pitch* and *fifteen-second commercial*. These are simply names for the way in which you introduce yourself. All X-CORPs should have their elevator pitches down pat. An online search for the term *elevator pitch* yields more than three million results. There are blogs, YouTube videos, and even complete books that have been written about the elevator pitch. It need not be difficult or complicated. Here's a straightforward exercise that will result in a short and pithy introduction: First, write down everything you want people to know about who you are, the "audience" you serve, what you do, and the value you bring to your clients. Next, highlight the key words. Finally, craft a couple of sentences using those words. Your goal is to make your introduction Twitter-like (about 12–15 words). Here are a few examples of powerful elevator pitches:

Hi, my name is Chris, and I own Midtown Body Shop. My shop serves the entire midtown area with collision-repair and auto-painting services that customers have been raving about for ten years.

Are you interested in better communication? I am Sandra Fisher and every year in Toastmasters I help hundreds of people improve their thinking, speaking and listening to ensure that their communication is the best it can be.

Good morning, I am Nancy Brown. I am a money manager who helps people reduce their tax burdens (Nancy's hands are pushing down as this is said) *and increase their savings and investment returns* (Nancy's hands are palms up and raising up). *How can I help you with your financial life?*

I thoroughly enjoy my job because I can tell people where to put it. I am Peter Newell and am the manager of U-Store. We have clean, cool space to store your stuff. Come in to see how we can serve as extra space for your overflow.

And my new one:

I'm uniquely qualified to help my clients because I've overcome the struggle of building a successful referral-based business. I have figured out a formula that can help just about any former-corporate-employee-turned-small-business-owner to build a referral business with Awareness, Authenticity, Attraction and Action.

When you introduce yourself—whether to an individual or a group—you must own that introduction. First say your name. Here's a tip about telling people your name: when you say your name, pause between your first and last name so people can catch it. If they don't catch your name, they may not hear anything else you say. The words you use in your elevator pitch must be captivating for you. Ideally, your introduction will be so enthralling that you'll get a response like, "How do you do that?" Or "Tell me more." To that end, you may want to include a question in your pitch, especially if you can word it so the persons with whom you're speaking will think about how they can relate to your product or service. For example, if you sell business-related insurance, you may ask (as the last part of your elevator pitch), "I represent a lot of new products with substantially lower premiums. When was the last time you reviewed your businesses insurance?" Be prepared with a response. I've seen people with exceptional elevator pitches who have no idea what to say when asked a follow-up question. They can't seem to succinctly give more detail about their product or service. Determine exactly what it is that others should know about you, and then figure out how to say it in 3–4 sentences. Make it compelling so people will be willing to listen to you for a minute.

How Do People Talk About Your Business And How Can You Help Them To Talk About Your Business?

The way you talk about your business is the way other people will talk about your business. It's your PR. If you don't know what others are saying about you, then find out. Ask people whom you trust. You can ask, "If you were going to tell someone about my business, what would you say?" If it's difficult for someone to answer that question, then perhaps you're not saying enough about your business, or you're not saying it in a way that makes it easy for others to repeat. If you have a business coach, you can ask your coach to do a survey as I've done for many of my clients. One such client was a handyman, Jim, who could do just about anything, but his specialty was electrical work. When I asked Jim how his customers talk about his business, he said, "They love my work." We decided to confirm that theory, so Jim gave me the names of fifteen past customers. I called each of those past customers and asked the same two questions of each one:

What are the three things you like most about working with Jim?

What could Jim do better?

I discovered that while Jim's customers were happy with *his* work, they weren't happy with the roofer and the plumber to whom he had been referring his customers: The roofer did shoddy work and the plumber often no-showed, or when he did show up, his rates were exorbitant. Clients that had used Jim in the past (remember, they generally *loved* his work) still did not call him again when they needed handyman services, because of their negative experiences with those other companies referred by Jim. They thought less of Jim for having recommended the bad roofer and plumber. When I told him about my discovery, Jim was shocked. He had never checked on the roofer or the plumber. (They were members of his closed networking group—the type of group in which referrals are expected and required.) My client had the expectation that since the roofer and plumber belonged to his networking group, they would provide outstanding work and service to his customers. Unfortunately, that was not the case.

The good news is that Jim did a good job of "damage control." He got on the phone and called every one of his customers who'd ever had a problem, and told them he would make it right. His customers appreciated his concern, and this resulted in more referrals for him. In fact, Jim's business grew to the point where he had to hire two additional employees. By the way, after that incident, Jim found a new group of professionals to whom he could confidently refer his customers.

I've had to learn those same lessons myself: A computer geek messed up my client's computer system so badly that she nearly lost her business. A photographer, used by a member of my group, "lost" wedding photos and then disappeared, owing me a considerable amount of money. Of course, most members of closed networking groups provide good professional services to their (and your) clients. Still, you may need to do your homework to be sure those to whom you refer business are providing the same high level of service that you do. After all, it's *your* reputation that's on the line, so protect it!

When people experience your product or service, they will talk about you differently. Encourage your clients to talk about their experience with you and to spread the word. I like to ask my clients, "Would you be comfortable introducing me to some of your clients?" More often than not, they say yes and then ask me what they should say. I then teach them how to introduce me. You can do the same.

How Do You Want To Show Up?

Put your best foot forward when you meet with your clients or potential clients, and when you go to any type of function. If you show up as someone who is overwhelmed and tired, and who doesn't take care of themselves, no one will be eager to do business with you. Subconsciously, people don't want to add to your burden. Remember my story in Chapter One? I learned this the hard way. When you show up, *all* of you shows up: your physical self, your emotional self, your personal "vibe." Donna Daisy, Ph.D., Psychologist and author, advises, "Take responsibility for how you are showing up in this world." She cautions, "Your every word and action has a ripple effect that carries out into the world. Make conscious choices about all the details of your life: how you look at someone, the tone of voice you choose, whether you are compassionate or oblivious."[8] Regretfully, too many small business owners don't take Dr. Daisy's advice. At one early morning networking event I used to attend, one of the participants would always say, "I'm not a morning person. I'm so not a morning person." Not the best way to make a good impression. Represent yourself as the confident, dynamic person you are: Be on time and be prepared. If you feel you can't put your best foot forward—whatever the reason—it's better not to show up at all. Remember, you only get one chance to make a strong first impression. It can't be undone. No one is going to come up to you and say, "Hmmm…not putting your best foot forward this morning, are you?" They simply won't do business with you.

How Do People Perceive You?

What impression are you making? What do others take away from your interaction with them? In one of my networking groups, we have a "chatterer" whom I'll call Cathy. Immediately after each group member has introduced themselves—usually before they've even sat down—Chatty Cathy makes a comment about that person. Her comments are sometimes catty, sometimes snarky, and usually inappropriate. She thinks she's being funny and establishing camaraderie, but most of the group members simply think she's rude.

Ditch the Hat

Susie, a woman I see at many networking functions, owns a printing business. She used to show up at these events wearing a rather beat-up cowboy hat. A couple of years ago, Susie told me her business was falling short of her forecast by 25 percent. She asked to meet with me for an initial consultation. Sure enough, she showed up at our meeting sporting her hat.

In the middle of our session, Susie asked me what I thought about her hat. I responded, "I'm curious as to why you wear it." She told me she thought it would make her stand out. It was time for some tough love and honesty: I told her that in my mind, it did make her stand out, but unfortunately not in a good way. I asked Susie how she thought her customers, and those at networking events would answer her question. She reflected for a moment and then said, "Perhaps I need to rethink the hat."

How are you showing up? What kind of impression are you making? It's essential that you not only answer those questions yourself, but that you also get the opinions of others. Ask a trusted friend or coach—someone who will be totally honest with you. Ask yourself, "What is *my* hat?" Is it the clothes you wear at networking events? The way you answer the telephone? Your lack of follow-up? To answer truthfully requires courage and a willingness to take a good hard look at yourself.

Asking others how they see you (and your business) may take you out of your comfort zone, but it's vital. Gather your courage and be willing to "go there." Ask a few people you trust, "Is there anything I need to clean up or be aware of in terms of the conversation that's out there about me and my business? Am I creating a positive environment in how I talk about business?" You have to be willing to ask and willing to listen. Don't ask only those who will fluff your feathers. Change doesn't have to be monumental. It may be something simple, like not wearing a hat. Resolve to learn how you're being perceived, then make changes accordingly.

Remember—networking is making a connection and then nurturing a relationship from that connection. Prepare yourself for networking. Show up and be honest and open. Enjoy it. You'll become a networking super star and, invariably and amazingly, create success.

Nobody ever said, "Work ball!" They say, "Play ball!"
To me, that means having fun.

— Willie Stargell

CHAPTER EIGHT

THE LIST OF TEN

Your number one strategy

Building a referral-based business takes time, energy, effort, emotion and *a strategy*. It's not something that happens all by itself. So...how to begin? Start with your *List of Ten*. Simply put, this is a list of ten potential referral partners. Your list is comprised of the names of both people and businesses—that you may or may not know—who can add value to your business, *and* you can add value to theirs. Those on your List of Ten do not have to be former customers or clients. They may be some day, but that's not the point. Your referral sources will vary, but the bottom line is this: The relationship you have with your referral partners must be a win-win for both of you. They may indeed be past or present clients, but they could also be friends, family, and others with whom you have cultivated relationships. Your List of Ten should be your primary referral strategy.

The History Of The List Of Ten

Since the relationship with those on your List of Ten will be a win-win (a win for your referral partner and a win for you), it's crucial to know what you'll be bringing to the party. Here's how it started for me: When I returned to Florida from California and decided to get serious about building my business, I read every book and attended every class imaginable. In one class, the participants were asked to list ten people we'd like to meet. My list included the mayor of our town. The next step was to write next to each name the *value that we could bring to that person*. In other words, what would it mean for me to meet the mayor, and what would it mean for the mayor to meet me? As I began to prepare for an eventual meeting with the mayor, I wondered what value I could bring to her. As I did my homework, I learned the mayor was passionate about small business, so that gave me a clue as to how I would introduce myself to her. A month later, totally by chance, I met the mayor at a breakfast meeting. Because of the work I'd done in the class, I knew how to introduce myself to her. I walked up to her and said, "I'm Lorraine Lane. I work with small businesses, and my passion is to ensure that small businesses have every chance to stay in business." I saw the spark in her eye. The mayor then asked, "How do you do that?" We were off and running. Ultimately the mayor referred me to her operations person. I never did get business out of it, but I quickly realized how valuable it is to be prepared with knowing who you want to meet and why. I've refined the concept, christened it the List of Ten, and have been using it personally for over a decade. Of course, I use it with my clients as well.

How To Build Your List Of Ten

Since your List of Ten will eventually become the core of both your network and your networking activity, give it the consideration it deserves. Here's a list of questions that should spark ideas for individuals or organizations that can go on your list:

- Whom do I want to meet?

- To what type of business (or individual) can I add the most value?

- Who can add value to my business?

- Who is my ideal client?

- Who have been my best clients?

- What other individuals or companies might be similar to my best clients?

- Who's given me a terrific referral and may have other referrals for me?

A great way to begin creating your List of Ten is to brainstorm these questions with colleagues or your mastermind group. After brainstorming and coming up with a list, the next step is to block out some time on your calendar to work on your list. If you need more ideas, check out local business journals, Chamber of Commerce publications, business magazines such as *INC* and *Entrepreneur*, and any other local publications you can get your hands on. Be on the lookout for individuals or organizations that might be a good source of business for you. Add them to your list and write down why you are putting them on your list. Make note of the value you feel you can provide to them. Keep going through this process until you've created a targeted list that feels workable. ("Workable" means you're willing to take the necessary action to meet each and every individual on your list.)

Start Working Your List

With your List of Ten in hand, it's time to get to work—and get into action. Select one person from your list and make a commitment to meet that individual. Your meeting can be in person (certainly the best method) or through some form of technology. I recognize that you may not be able to hop on an airplane to meet far-off people in person, so you have other options for meeting with those on your List. Do your homework on this person so you can get to know the individual from a distance, and also discover how you might meet him or her:

- Google this person.

- Search for this person on LinkedIn.

- Search for a Facebook business page.

- Find out which local organizations this person might participate in.

- Does this person have a website? If so, check it out.

- Perhaps this person makes public appearances? If so, where?

- Do you know someone who might know this person?

Putting yourself in a situation where you will be able to meet this person is something you will need to choreograph. Of course, there's the option of contacting the individual yourself, but before you do....

Prepare For Your First Meeting

Before putting yourself in a situation in which you're likely to meet someone on your List of Ten, make sure you're fully prepared by answering the following:

- What value do you bring?

- What will you say?

- How will you invite further interaction?

Understand the value you can bring to this person. Practice what you will say and determine ahead of time how you will continue the conversation. A little role-playing might be fun and helpful. Find a friend who can play the part of the person you'll be meeting. Try it both ways, too. You can play the part of the person you'll be meeting to gain additional insight, and maybe hear some good conversation ideas from your friend (who's playing you). I've done this myself, and I can tell you the results have often been phenomenal. A little practice in advance makes for a much more powerful presentation on your part when the real meeting takes place.

Meeting a Professor

In one of my recent ten-week A-Game programs, I requested a volunteer, "Who would like help on making contact with someone on your List of Ten?" John, a divorce coach, stepped up to the plate, explaining that he was keen to meet a professor—whose expertise was relationships—at a local university. When I asked what value John could bring to this professor, he couldn't answer, so we brainstormed. We determined John could offer the professor a different type of audience and a different forum in which to share his expertise.

John had been hoping that someone in one of his networking groups knew this professor and would make an introduction for him. I suggested John simply call the professor and introduce himself. The idea of a "cold call," was a bit scary, but now that John was clear on the value he could provide to the professor, he agreed to make the call. He waited until late on a Friday afternoon, hoping the professor would have left for the day. To his surprise, she picked up the phone. The call went extremely well, and they chatted for quite a while. Each of them was excited about the other's work. The professor invited John to an event as her guest. The attendees at this event were all relationship experts. This was an event that John would otherwise never have attended. John invited the professor to be a guest speaker on a teleseminar he was hosting. She was thrilled to have a new audience with which to share her passion. The bottom line was that each provided real value for the other: benefits that could not have been imagined prior to making the connection.

Had John waited to meet someone who could introduce him to the professor, he may never have met her, and never enjoyed the outstanding work they did together. You are your own best referral source. Do your homework. Understand the value you bring.

Cultivate Your List Of Ten

If you happen to enjoy gardening, you know you can't just throw seeds on the ground and expect them to grow. You must first prepare the soil, carefully plant the seeds, and then take good care of those seeds. Only then will they grow. It's the same with the relationships you develop with those on your List of Ten. I am constantly cultivating my relationships with my List of Ten. I recently spent an entire day helping someone on my List of Ten prepare a proposal for his business. I didn't charge him: It was part of the give and take of our relationship. Another individual on my List of Ten asked if I could help her with her resume. I was delighted to. I'm now doing business with her new company.

How can you cultivate relationships with your List of Ten? Here are seven ways to acknowledge your referral partners:

1. Read newspapers and magazines with a different mindset. Are there articles that might be of interest to someone on your list? When you find something, share it. A simple note, "Here's something I thought might interest you," with an article attached will be welcomed.

2. Recognize notable dates such as birthdays and anniversaries.

3. Invite someone on your list to be your guest at a special event.

4. Subscribe to a magazine for someone on your list, or purchase a book as a gift.

5. Ask for advice. In general, people love to help others. Many people will freely share brilliant ideas and the wisdom they've gathered over their years in business, and feel honored that you asked. As a result, your relationship will deepen.

6. Send a handwritten thank-you note with a $10 gift card.

7. Hold a holiday open house at your place of business.

Taking the time to cultivate relationships with those on your List of Ten will reward you a thousand times over. Business will flow because you've made the effort to strengthen these ties. Once the people on your list get to know and trust you, and understand your business and the value you bring to them, they will happily refer you to others. I've been cultivating my List of Ten for ten years. Nine times out of ten, when someone on my List of Ten sends me a referral, it turns into a piece of business.

I don't want to entirely discount "regular" networking. We're going to talk about that aspect of business-building in the next chapter. Just be sure that you use the powerful List of Ten strategies I've outlined in this chapter before moving on. Implementing your own List of Ten plan will boost your business—perhaps to the point that any other networking would simply be a waste of time. Still, if you've done your "ten" and are hungry for more, move on to the next chapter for another trip to the networking buffet.

Whoever said,
"It's not whether you win or lose that counts,"
probably lost.

— Martina Navratilova

CHAPTER NINE

TRADITIONAL NETWORKING
Sometimes you just gotta get out there…

We've talked about building your network the A-Game way. When you play the A-Game, you will become a networking super star and generate business-building referrals. We've discussed your List of Ten, your primary strategy for building a referral-based business. There is a time and a place for "traditional" networking: attending networking meetings and functions. Traditional networking can be an excellent way for you to gain visibility with your intended target market. Let's take a look at traditional networking and how it fits into your strategy for building a referral-based business.

Networking Groups

Any time business people come together to talk about what they do, to exchange ideas, suggestions, and to help each other find more business, that's a "networking" meeting. Some gatherings include networking as a portion of the overall meeting agenda, like a local Chamber of Commerce, but there are also groups that meet with the specific goal of helping group members grow their businesses through exchanging potential leads and new customer information. Those groups include BNI, NPI and others. They meet on a weekly basis, usually early in the morning.

These groups, referred to as *networking and referral groups,* are closed to non-members. You may already be a member of this specific type of group. One of the leading selling points of these groups is that they are usually limited in membership, so there is only one member from any particular type of business: one plumber, one attorney, one dentist, etc. That's to prevent competition among group members and encourage members to help each other grow their businesses. A typical group may be comprised of approximately 20 members. Members typically arrive for open networking (chatting among themselves) about 30 minutes prior to the start of the formal meeting. Once the formal part of the meeting begins, reports are given by the president, secretary and treasurer. Next, all members give very short introductory speeches that let others know who they are and a bit about their business offerings.

The group then engages in the nuts and bolts portion of the meeting: the exchange of leads among members. As different group members go about their days, they may meet someone who expresses a need for a particular kind of business, service or product. For example, I may be in the landscaping business. When I chat with a customer, she tells me she's on the hunt for a good plumber to do some work around her house. I'm not in the plumbing business, but through my referral group, I know someone who is. At the next meeting, I'll give the plumber in my group (assuming there is one) the contact ("lead") information for my customer (after getting her permission, of course).

As members share leads, those leads are usually recorded by the group secretary, or other officer, for record-keeping purposes and follow-up. If you were given a referral during the previous week's meeting, you're expected to report on that referral. Some groups have a requirement that members share a certain minimum number of leads per month. Missing that goal may end up having your business placed on probation.

These types of networking groups often rely on the Rule of 250: the assumption that every member knows at least 250 people, and each of those people also know 250, and so on. So, if each networking group member's Rolodex contains 250 contacts, you should be leaving every meeting with loads of referrals that'll have you rolling in the dough in no time, right? I hate to be the one to put the skids on your dreams but, unfortunately, the Rule of 250 rarely works out that way. Not everyone in a group member's Rolodex will be part of your target market – and not every group member is going to be willing to introduce you to the entire contents of his or her Rolodex. Simply put, success with these types of networking groups can be hit or miss.

The other type of networking group is an open networking meeting such as Chamber of Commerce meetings and other Business After Hours gatherings. In the Tampa Bay area where I live, the Tampa Bay Business Journal holds open networking meetings. My advice is to do some homework (online searches, business news sections of newspapers, etc.) to learn about the networking meetings that are held in your area. At a large Chamber of Commerce Business After Hours meeting, there may be as many as 250 attendees. I'm on the Board of Directors of my local Chamber of Commerce, so I attend many the Business After Hours meetings. Over the years, I've witnessed (more often than not) that attendees arrive and…

- go to the bar to grab a drink, and then sit at a table for the rest of the evening.

or…

- look for their friends—who have often saved a seat for them—then sit and chat with the people they already know for the duration of the event.

By now, you know exactly what's wrong with this picture. There's no networking happening. None. Zero. Nada. Does this make sense? (Answer: not if you want to build your business.) Networking isn't about making new friends or meeting with old friends. Make a lunch or dinner date if you want to spend time social time with your acquaintances. Remember, *networking is making a connection and then creating and nurturing a relationship from that connection* The purpose of attending a networking meeting is to make *yourself and your business visible*. And effective networking takes planning.

The Real Purpose Of Networking

When you think about it, networking is nothing new. As children, we learned to network with our friends in the neighborhood. Our parents gave us the social skills we needed to "play nice" with others. Part of that certainly included important life-skills like sharing, a willingness to help and contribute, and to "show up" for life. Thanks Mom! That willingness to be helpful is a central aspect of our business-oriented networking and marketing activities. Our goal should be to help others move forward and also to get some credit for it for ourselves. This is not selfish in any way; we're helping first, getting recognition (and hopefully a bit of business) later. The most successful business owners I've met help others to succeed. They share information freely and consistently demonstrate their level of integrity through their relationships.

Do a self-check of your own priorities. Do you genuinely care about helping to fill the needs of others in a networking group? If not, there's no reason for you to attend. If you're going to networking meetings for the right reasons and with the right attitude, you'll have a great deal to offer the group. Whenever you encounter a new face, whether in your networking group or in a social situation, it's always important to nurture a solid relationship based on mutual respect and caring. If you take the time to get to know someone, to learn about their needs, you may be able to assist that person in the future. Remember: Networking is about making connections. Everything else is secondary. You can't help anyone if you don't connect with them first. Perhaps you've attended a Chamber of Commerce networking breakfast, where you shake a few members' hands, meet a few of the guests, enjoy a cup of coffee and then leave. If so, you passed up a golden opportunity to create a "networking moment" because you failed to connect with anyone–and networking is about making *connections*.

How Do You Connect?

So, how do you connect? First, keep in mind that networking is a skill that grows through practice, so attending networking events on a regular basis and meeting people is important. I always tell my clients: You don't *have* to network. You *get the opportunity* to network. Two different mindsets and two different types of energy are involved. Face it. Most people don't like to be *forced* to do anything, so if you go into a networking event feeling as if you have to be there, people are going to sense your frustration; but if you develop the attitude that you're realizing a wonderful opportunity to meet new people and expand your list of contacts, people will pick up on your positive mindset and energy. Armed with the right attitude, you'll find that regularly attending networking events will help you keep in touch with people you want to influence, and more than a few individuals will be ready and willing to help you when the time is right.

As part of your networking, make it a point to seek out new contacts. Decide for yourself and your situation: It could be one per week or a dozen a month. Invest quality time in your networking. Build your relationships by fully understanding what you have to offer and then network with realistic expectations. You won't land that $250,000 contract as a result of a five-minute engagement. The fact is it takes up to ten (or more) positive encounters to begin to trust a new contact. So be patient: It usually takes some time to experience the results of your networking efforts. For instance, I've been a member of my local Chamber of Commerce for more than eight years. I've served on various committees and the Board of Directors, and I've offered numerous workshops on behalf of the Chamber. Last month, a business owner called to meet with me. He said, "I am seeking you out because I've watched you over the years and appreciate how professional you are. I know you have lots of good experience and knowledge that will help me and my business." It takes time to build that kind of trust. Of course, there are exceptions: When done with intention and the "power of attraction," it's highly possible to move quickly into doing business with a new contact just because you showed up at the right time and place and were prepared. Here are a few strategies for making your networking work:

- Know as much as you can about the people who will be at the event and have 2-3 people in mind who you would like to meet.

- When possible, go to networking meetings alone. I know, it's so much easier when you have a buddy to lean on. If you do carpool, agree in advance to spread out. If you are alone, chances are that more people will connect with you.

- Have you ever noticed that some people stand near the registration table and greet you in those precious moments before you start weaving your way to the refreshment table or start to network? This is an excellent strategy, if only because you're getting people as they're coming in, looking for someone to talk to and connect with. Be the first person with whom they connect.

- Be a "connector." Move around and introduce people to each other.

- Remember my nerve calming strategy: Find the person who is more uncomfortable than you and make sure they feel welcome. Sit between people you don't know. If you sit next to someone you already know, you won't be forming a new relationship–and that's the purpose of attending networking events, isn't it?

- Sorry, but don't attend networking events to eat. You are there to connect, not eat. Focus on people, not food.

- Create space to catch a person's name. If you're good with names, then great. If not, check online for tricks and techniques for remembering names and faces. Practice saying your name so that others will catch it. Here's one of my favorite tricks: Say your first name, then pause slightly before saying your last name. The pause creates the space for the listener to capture your first name and not be distracted that they didn't get it. If you didn't catch someone's name, ask the person to repeat it. Then you repeat it, so you hear it said again.

- Ladies, when I go to networking events, I don't carry my purse. If I will need money, it goes into my jacket pocket along with my business cards. This is so freeing, and I highly recommend it.

- No chewing gum. Need I say more?

- Develop your questioning skills. Find ways to encourage people to talk about their business. They will see you as an interesting person although they've been talking about themselves. Funny how that works, but it works exceedingly well.

- "Good questions are far more difficult than good answers." (Persian proverb)

- When I first started my HR job as a recruiter in Corporate America, I learned quickly that I didn't ask enough questions. I developed an extensive file of questions that I still use today. Questions fascinate me. I've recently read that a skill that is valued in leaders today is the ability to ask insightful questions.

- Asking powerful, insightful questions is only half the equation. The ability to *listen* is probably even more valuable. Listen as if your life depends on it, because your business life does. Practice being totally present with the person with whom you're interacting. There is no more precious gift than feeling heard.

I could go on, but there are so many books about networking that you can spend the rest of your life reading them and never finish. The way to become a networking super star is to practice, practice, practice.

Like life, basketball is messy and unpredictable.
It has its way with you, no matter how hard you try to control it.
The trick is to experience each moment with a clear mind and open heart.
When you do that, the game – and life – will take care of itself.

—Phil Jackson

CONCLUSION

Welcome to the big leagues! You now have the tools to bring your A-Game to your business each and every day, and to become a networking super star. You've done a good job getting this far, but you're just getting started. As a small business owner, you are not alone: There are 23 million small businesses in America, which account for 54 percent of all U.S. sales. The number of small businesses in the United States has increased 49 percent since 1982.[9] Note: every country has its own definition of what constitutes a small business, and it varies widely. Small businesses make significant contributions to the economy of the U.S. There's more good news: According to statistics published by the Small Business Administration (SBA), seven out of ten new employer establishments survive at least two years and 51 percent survive at least five years. This is a far cry from the previous long-held belief that 50 percent of businesses fail in the first year, and 95 percent fail within five years.

There are many reasons small businesses fail. One of the primary reasons for failure is low sales. I sincerely believe if you play the A-Game of Referrals, if you bring your A-Game to your business each and every day, and if you become a networking super star, then low sales will not be a concern for you and your small business. I've provided you with the tools you need for business-building referrals. From my own experience and that of my clients, I know that these tools work. It's now up to you to get off the couch and get into the game. I encourage you to plan your strategy for business-building referrals and fully embrace you're A-Game. After all, it's your game. Play to win.

ACKNOWLEDGEMENTS

The idea of writing a book has been germinating for more than a decade. If I had one dollar for every time a participant in my A-Game Program suggested that I write a book, I'd have quite a nice bank account. Writing a book is not a solo endeavor. I'd like to especially thank the following people:

- My parents, for instilling basic networking skills in me (and my brothers, Jim and Paul) from the very start. We were taught to be polite, to say please and thank you, and cautioned not to chew gum in public. My Dad never had good things to say about gum chewers—something about looking like cows chewing their cud. Some lessons are never forgotten! The skills I learned as a child have been repurposed and have become the building blocks for my success. Thanks, Mom and Dad, for raising me in a way that helped succeeding in business come naturally.

- My clients. Through the years, I have been fortunate to work with countless men and women who have enriched my work and my life.

- My coach, Dave Buck, who has helped me succeed at every turn and who reminds me to bring my A-Game to every undertaking.

- All the players of the A-Game program: We've learned along the way and played the A-Game of referrals with blood, sweat and tears.

- Valerie Taloni, for her tenacious questioning and insightful conversations. Without her writing skills, this book would still be a distant dream of *I'll write a book one day*. She brought to life ideas that—until now—had no voice.

- Everyone who has provided insight in some way, simply because our paths crossed.

- My daughter, Liz, for her "you can do it, Mom" encouragement.

- And last, but not for a moment least, my grandson, Brady, whom I call "the Mayor." He's a four-year-old who networks like a pro: He greets the cashiers at the grocery store and they run to get him balloons. He doesn't hide behind his parents with shyness. He has observed his parents and their conversational skills and he is the beneficiary of their grace. I've learned many a business lesson from this four-year-old!

ABOUT THE AUTHOR

An ex-corporate-employee-turned-small-business owner, Lorraine Lane is a networking super star and a walking billboard for *Business-Building Referrals*: more than eighty percent of her business comes from referrals. Lorraine works with small business owners coaching them one-on-one to build their businesses, and facilitates the A-Game, a ten-week program in the art and strategy of building a business through referrals. A marketing specialist, Lorraine brings more than two decades of experience to her work. She coaches small business owners helping them build referral-based businesses, and facilitates the A-Game, a ten-week program in the art and strategy of building a business through referrals. Her ideal clients are X-CORPs, ex-corporate-employees-turned-small-business-owners, who want and need to build their businesses or find themselves overwhelmed, frustrated, and in crisis-management mode. After a long and successful career as a corporate human resources manager, Lorraine became an X-CORP. She brings more than two decades of learning and experience to her individual clients and A-Game Program participants. Having started her own consulting business in Florida, California, and then Florida again, Lorraine understands the issues faced by entrepreneurs, and knows first-hand what it takes to build a small business.

Lorraine's background includes an undergraduate degree in Education from the University of Vermont, and a Masters in Business Administration. Lorraine served as an adjunct faculty member for San Jose State University's Professional Development Center and now serves in that capacity for a local university and community college in the Tampa area.

Having served in leadership positions with various Chambers of Commerce, Lorraine is a current member of the Board of Directors for the Central Pasco Chamber of Commerce. She recently received the Chamber Member of the Year award and The President's Award.

Lorraine lives in the Tampa area, where it is sunny and warm. When she's not playing the A-Game and building her business with referrals, Lorraine enjoys cooking, games, reading great books, and spending time with Brady, her four-year-old grandson, whose imagination knows no limits.

CONTACT THE AUTHOR

Lorraine Lane welcomes your emails and phone calls.

Email: Lorraine@BusinessBuildingReferrals.com

Telephone: 813-402-6224

www.BusinessBuildingReferrals.com

(ENDNOTES)

1. © Jeff Klein, author of *Working for Good* and *It›s Just Good Business.* Quoted with permission.

2. *Heart, Smarts, Guts and Luck,* Anthony K. Tijan, Richard J. Harrington, Tsun-Yan Hsieh, Harvard Business Review Press, 2012

3. http://hbr.org/2005/01/managing-oneself/ar/1

4. Quoted with permission. LindaStone.net

5. *The Seven Habits of Highly Effective People,* Stephen R. Covey, Simon & Schuster, 1989

6. Source: *Human Motivation,* David C. McClelland, Cambridge University Press, 1988

7. http://dictionary.reference.com/browse/networking?s=t

8. Donna Daisy, Ph.D., psychologist, author and motivational speaker

9. http://www.sba.gov

Made in the USA
San Bernardino, CA
13 April 2014